DEAR JEFF

DEAR JEFF

An Older Brother's Straightforward Advice
on Preparing to Enter the Temple

J WASHBURN

POST TENEBRAS LVX

Who is J Washburn?

Born in Page, Arizona, practically on the Navajo Reservation, and raised in Idaho with his several siblings, J began writing stories when he was about three. When he wasn't writing, he spent his childhood living the adventures described in his books. He earned a Bachelor of English from Brigham Young University–Idaho and a Master of English from Brigham Young University. Aspiring to be a renaissance man, he has worked as a lawn mower, a concrete pourer, a street preacher, a meta-physicist, a typographer, a graphic designer, a usability designer, a warrior poet, and even an English teacher. He also suffers from chronic somnia.

What kind of a name is J?

(Okay, moving to first-person now.)

No, I'm not trying to copy J.R.R. Tolkien or J.K. Rowling. J really is my first name—my whole first name.

Nope, not J-A-Y. Not J with a period (abbreviating it actually makes it longer). It starts and ends with J.

Just J.

An interesting side note: if you throw a pen at a paper from at least five feet away, it nearly always spells my name.

"But what kind of a name is J?"—you're still asking. Well, I'll tell you. There was once a man named Melvin J. Ballard (whose middle name was Joseph, but he liked to abbreviate it). My grandpa was named J Ballard Washburn in honor of this man. But he just got the J (without the period). I was named after my grandpa, and I just got his J.

Which is nice.

After all, brevity is the soul of wit.

Was J the only letter involved?

No, not at all. I'm indebted to many people who helped me write this book.

I owe a legendary grandpa, an exemplary older brother, and two goodly parents. I owe a mission president who stuck to the Coke side of the law and believed in free will. I owe mission companions who sought learning by study and also by faith. I owe many leaders and mentors, including a New Testament teacher who respectfully didn't shy from the mysteries and a seminary teacher whose heart was pure enough to complete the grail quest.

I also owe my alpha, beta, and gamma readers—this would be an awful book without them. In fact, I'd like to thank them by name: Jim, Sonya, Jeff, Jax, Abe, Tevya, Sean, Joel, Stephanie, Jessica, Kim, Krista, Ashley, Ann, and Bunny.

And I thank the readers at MormonLifeHacker.com for contributing to the gospel conversation and sharing it with the world.

Most of all, I want to thank the poor wayfaring man of grief. He sweat blood for me, and the grace that came is what really made this book—the final result being far beyond my mere capacity.

How can someone contact J?

If you want to make history (we're talking second edition here), find a mistake and submit it to typos@jwashburn.com (and make sure to mention this book's title).

If you want to contact me personally, go to JWashburn.com.

To Tev

who led me.

CONTENTS

ENDOWMENT 89

Sealing   171

Afterthoughts   191

If thou shalt ask, thou shalt receive revelation upon revelation, knowledge upon knowledge, that thou mayest know the mysteries and peaceable things—that which bringeth joy, that which bringeth life eternal.

— *Doctrine and Covenants 42:61*

DEAR JEFF

An Older Brother's Straightforward Advice
on Preparing to Enter the Temple

J WASHBURN

Our God is a consuming fire.

INTRODUCTION

We ask thee, Holy Father, that thy servants may go forth from this house armed with thy power, and that thy name may be upon them, and thy glory be round about them, and thine angels have charge over them.

— *Doctrine and Covenants 109:22*

1. Devotion

As you know, Jeff, when I was in D.C. last Christmas, I toured the George Washington Masonic Memorial. And, as I did, I honestly considered becoming a Mason.

I couldn't help it.

Maybe I've over-romanticized it, but wouldn't it be awesome to be part of a united body that works against the forces that plague mankind?

Truth is, it wasn't the first time I'd had a thought like that. I've never really admitted this out loud, but even when I was a kid I wanted to be a Jedi, dressed in black, just like Luke Skywalker. And I'm not talking about being a Jedi in a galaxy far, far away. I wanted to be a Jedi in *this* world, right here. I wanted to pay the price of devotion and self-denial till I could control the weak-minded or do trick flips off an execution plank. I wanted to have that same physical, mental, and spiritual focus.

As I passed through my teenage years, this same type of secret desire made me wonder if I could join the Tibetan monks (yes, really)—to own nothing more than a red robe and walk barefoot toward inner peace and actual enlightenment. I longed, and still long, to achieve that commitment.

In college, I secretly admired Silas, the albino extremist from *The DaVinci Code*. Not that I wanted to be a bad guy, but I envied his sheer *devotion*—he was so committed to Opus Dei that he tortured himself with a spiked cilice around his thigh as both a reminder and a proof of his dedication. I respected that. I wished I could love as fully as he hated.

And as I walked through that Masonic temple in D.C., it hit me that the Masons might be one way to pay that fuller devotion—like joining the Jedi order but in real life. I'm telling you this story about the Masons, Jeff, because it illustrates my longing. Maybe you've felt that way too, this desire to be committed to something higher and purer.

But I admit my longing seems a little contradictory: I belong to the best of mortal organizations—the church Christ himself set up—and yet, for some reason, I'm still on the lookout for something more, as if Christ's church asks too little of me. (I have to mention that the church may be led by God, but that doesn't mean there aren't some mortal flaws in the output because, just like any good teacher, God lets his students learn by doing, which sometimes means making mistakes—and here ends the first of many tangents.)

What it boils down to, though, is that I can't muster the *devotion* I feel I ought to have. The main commandment—the *great* commandment—is to love God with all your heart, might, mind, and strength. In other words, fully devoted to divinity. This isn't just saying your heart needs to be in the right place. It's saying your body does too. It's about physical fitness, but it's also about intellectual, social, and spiritual fitness. It's loving God with all of these—loving God wholly. And I'm not there yet. And because I'm not there yet, I still feel that longing, the feeling that drives me to keep reaching.

But even though I haven't been able to muster full devotion, I'm already in an organization—Christ's own church—that helps me to do this. I just haven't leveled-up enough to earn that spiritual blackbelt or the red Tibetan robe.

The temple is the center of a higher order within Christ's organization. The temple is a pathway. It's a teaching tool. It gives us understanding. It's also a divine sanctuary that imbues us with the Spirit—puts it inside us—a spirit that helps us follow what we know. In other words, the temple gives us the knowledge we need to be more devoted, but it also gives us the spiritual gumption—what we need on the *inside*—to be more devoted. The temple gives access to the devotion I've sought for so long.

And that's why I'm writing this book to you—to help you prepare to join this order and walk this same way.

Unfortunately, they don't hand out lightsabers at the temple. (Not that I don't think they could—don't forget the cherubim's fiery swords.) What the temple offers is less flashy, but of much greater value: The temple helps us fully devote ourselves—to more completely obey that first and great commandment.

2. Don't Panic

Our guide led us upward through that Masonic tower, telling us cool facts about each room—one of which was a replica of the Masonic hall Washington himself presided in. I tried to get our guide to tell us about the hidden parts, but she had a pretty good excuse not to: "I'm not a Mason, and couldn't be if I wanted to—it's for males only. So I'll tell you as much as I know, but I'm an outsider just like all of you." And then she'd try to answer my questions, but it was never enough. And the more we saw, the more I felt I didn't get the full picture. As I walked between paintings and statues of Washington in his Masonic apron and sash,

I wanted to look him right in the eye and demand, *"What is it you're not telling me?"*

So there I was, considering joining this organization because I wanted to do a little more good, and yet I had no way of knowing what that organization looked like from the inside. So how could I know if I actually wanted in?

At the end of the tour, I stood on the balcony of the 333-foot tower, with powerful winds trying to push me over as I looked out across the vast, tiny city of D.C., and my question for George kept ringing in my head: "What is it you're not telling me?" I hated that feeling of not knowing—like the Masons were collectively looking at me and snickering. And not knowing what I would be getting into was enough to keep me from getting into it (at least so far).

Sometimes people have that same sort of experience with the temple. In fact, a good friend of mine wrote,

> My first time through left me frustrated for multiple reasons. First, you're told you'll be making the most important covenants of your life, yet you're not allowed to know what they are until you're making them. Second, nobody ever told me how ritualistic it was going to be... and it definitely took me by surprise. If I could recommend one thing, it would be to demystify the experience. I don't feel like anybody ever did that for me, and it would have been nice... so nothing catches you by surprise.

This type of comment is somewhat common. The first time to the temple has been frustrating for a lot of people (though that's certainly not true for everyone). Because of that, I almost think this book, like *The Hitchhiker's Guide*

to the Galaxy, needs the words DON'T PANIC inscribed across the front. There shouldn't be any panic—before, during, or after. And the cure is simply understanding.

If I didn't know what was coming, I probably would have even felt panic about baptism—someone dunking you in a font while a bunch of people watch. Looking at an ordinance as an isolated physical act makes it seem silly. But when it's connected to a deeper tradition with a host of symbols surrounding it, it's natural and expected.

Hopefully this book will reveal the deeper tradition and the host of symbols, demystifying the temple experience so that you don't find yourself saying, "What is it you're not telling me?" I don't want you to feel that. So I'll explain as much as I can, as well as I can.

3. DEAR JEFF

As you know, a few years ago I was hired to read Grandpa's journals and then write up his personal history (which increased my vigor for journaling—I'll tell you that).

Even though he was a busy physician, missionary, and dad, he always set high marks for his temple attendance—a certain number of sessions per year—which he'd record in his journal. I was surprised by how often he attended. But he surprised me even more when he would increase those numbers in consecutive years. I guess the moral of the story is that we ought to attend often, maybe more than we think.

His example inspired me to set my own high marks, and as I attended more, I thought about the temple more. That, connected with the additional journaling, resulted in a long temple notebook where I collected several years worth of study. When Sioux began preparing for her mission to Korea, she wanted to learn about the temple in a more candid way—from one of her own siblings. So she asked if I'd have a few temple talks with her before she received her endowment. Those discussions helped me realize the need for a book like you're reading now.

I don't expect this to be the last book on the temple you'll ever read. Prophets have written on this topic, and if I were trying to rival them, I'd be doomed. Instead, I have—well, not the *advantage*, but simply—the *vantage* of being lowly: I'm just your brother. But not having the mantle of apostleship lets me speak less formally. I'll echo what prophets have taught, but I'll speak candidly too—not in a watered-down way, but in a milk-before-meat sort of way, giving you easier access to one of the best things we mortals can have.

And, Jeff, as you read, remember to focus on the scriptures and what the Spirit teaches you. Those will both be a lot more important than my words.

Speaking of what we learn from the Lord—he warned us about how we ought to respect things like that:

> Remember that that which cometh from above is sacred, and must be spoken with care, and by constraint of the Spirit. (D&C 63:64)

The temple is a sacred topic, so I'll have to be careful. There may be moments where you feel I'm saying a little too little, but that's because I'm taking that scripture as my commission, and I want to tread with care.

I just want you to know what to expect in this book.

And now that you know the purpose, the source, and the tone, you should know the content: It will cover the temple ceremonies, which Joseph Smith described as instruction on

> the principles and order of the Priesthood, attending to washings, anointings, endowments and communication of keys pertaining to the Aaronic Priesthood, and so on to the highest order of the Melchizedek Priesthood, setting forth the order pertaining to the Ancient of Days, and all those plans and principles by which any one is enabled to secure the fullness of those blessings which have been prepared for the Church.

Joseph explained that because they were sacred they were "to be received only by the spiritual minded." And, although these things were initially given to a limited number, they would eventually "be made known to all the Saints of the last days, so soon as they are prepared to receive" (*History of the Church* 5:2). This book is about preparing to receive.

I see this as a 6-day, 12-day, or 18-day course, depending on how much time and devotion you have to spare. You could spend one day apiece on the six main chapters. And you could expand that by spending a day apiece on the 12 reading assignments (a sermon and a scripture are attached to each chapter). Just take it at whatever pace you feel is best. I'm a big fan of slow and steady. But remember the key to slow and steady is *steady*—make sure you keep coming back.

Most people don't do any sort of serious temple study until a few weeks (or even days) before they go. You're much younger though, which gives you the advantage of letting what you learn marinate for a couple years—so the ideas really sink in. Also, it wouldn't be a bad idea to read this again in a year—I guarantee you'll get more out of it the second time.

And, Jeff, I may be publishing this for whoever wants to read it (because I think it could help others), but it's really for you. I hope you'll find value in it.

It's also for you, Jax—so I'm glad you're reading too. And, by the way, thirteen isn't too young. Joseph Smith was about your age when he prayed for answers out loud for the first time.

To wrap up this little introduction, I want to share a scripture that connects all this together. This is what Abraham wrote in his temple journal nearly 4,000 years ago:

> And, finding <u>there was greater happiness and peace and rest for me</u>, I sought for the blessings of the fathers, and the right whereunto I should be ordained to administer the same; having been myself a follower of righteousness, <u>desiring also to be one who possessed great knowledge</u>, and to be a greater follower of righteousness... and to be a father of many nations, <u>a prince of peace</u>, and desiring to receive instructions, <u>and to keep the commandments of God</u>, I became a rightful heir, a High Priest, holding the right belonging to the fathers. (Abraham 1:2)

Grandpa's example did this for me—made me want greater happiness and peace, which in turn encouraged me to seek for it. And now I want to share with you some of what I've found.

4. PERSONAL STUDY

Each chapter ends with a Personal Study section. You may need to save these for your second time through this book—but don't put them off forever, especially the scriptural ones.

This first recommendation is the simplest:

- Read the official publication on Temples of the Church of Jesus Christ of Latter-day Saints

Go to jwashburn.com/books/dearjeff for links to download or purchase a copy.

PREPARATION

Lord, who shall abide in thy tabernacle? Who shall dwell in thy holy hill? He that walketh uprightly, and worketh righteousness, and speaketh the truth in his heart.

— *Psalms 15:1-2*

5. Worthy to Enter

Likely at some point or another, a friend of yours is going to ask you (a little offended, maybe—as if it were partially your decision) why you keep what's inside the temple a secret—and keep everyone else out.

You can tell him or her that there's no secret at all. In fact, we invite everyone to come. More than that, we send thousands of missionaries all over the world—you're going to be one of them in a couple of years. People think the goal is baptism, and that's often the phase investigators reach while missionaries are working with them. But the real purpose is to help people come closer to Christ, and baptism is just the first part. The temple is the last step, and people sometimes forget about it. But that's really what you'll be inviting people toward. So we're not trying to keep people out. Quite the opposite, in fact.

We invite everyone to come, but we don't let them in right away. That's where *worthiness* comes in. It's a word that isn't used much these days. Being worthy just means you've met certain qualifications. It means you've completed the *prerequisites*. It's the same thing that happens when you have to take Physics 218 and 318 before they'll let you in to 418. It's not that they don't want you to take it. They just want you to be ready for it when you do—so you'll actually benefit from it.

6. The Place of No Thorns

One of my favorite poems, an Irish song by Thomas Moore called "The Minstrel Boy," is about a young bard who goes to war and gets killed in battle:

> The minstrel boy to the war is gone,
> In the ranks of death you'll find him;
> His father's sword he hath girded on,
> His wild harp slung behind him;
> "Land of Song!" said the warrior bard,
> "Tho' all the world betray thee,
> One sword, at least, thy rights shall guard,
> One faithful harp shall praise thee!"

> The minstrel fell, but the foeman's chains
> could not drag his proud soul under:
> The harp he loved never spoke again,
> for he tore its chords asunder,
> and said, "No chains, shall sully thee,
> thou soul of love and bravery;
> thy songs were made for the pure and free
> and shall never sound in slavery."

Rather than let his harp be ravaged by the hands of the

enemy, the boy cut it to pieces—he destroyed it. With this act, he showed us an interesting perspective on the sacred. In this case, it was better for the sacred thing to be destroyed than to let it be profaned. It wasn't because he was jealous of his enemy, but because he loved his harp—it was his heart and soul. And can you imagine destroying something you loved so much? But with his last ounce of strength he cut it to pieces. "Thy songs were made for the pure and free," he said. And if the harp were used in slavery, it's essence would be destroyed, even if the physical part wasn't.

Let me take a moment for a bit of an extended metaphor to help clarify what I'm driving at. Imagine you live in a fantasy land—you're the hero that carries a sword and saves the princess with your boomerang.

An evil force has spread across the land—dark thorns growing on everything—through the grass, on rocks and trees, choking out flowers and birds, and crawling onto the skin and faces of people. And it's infectious, spreading to anything it gets close to.

So the forces of good get together and start burning away the thorns till they have cleared one small area on the map. They label this "the place of no thorns." And now that it's been purified, people can go there and feel safe from infection.

If you have a thorn on you and you walk into "the place of no thorns," you've immediately destroyed the essence of the whole place. It's no longer "the place of no thorns." Of course, the physical setting, the terrain and whatnot, hasn't changed one bit. But by entering it with thorns on you, you've made it so the place no longer exists. In fact, it's a metaphysical paradox: A place with a thorn in it can't simultaneously be a place without thorns—it's a contradiction.

Real life is not far from this fairy tale. Our world is a crazy place. "We wrestle not against flesh and blood, but against principalities, against powers, against the rulers of the darkness of this world, against spiritual wickedness in high places" (Ephesians 6:12). So instead of thorns, we have the powers of darkness around us. They're real, and, therefore, our battle against them and our eventual escape from them are real too. As these forces swirl around us, they pull this way and that, trying to get us to spend our attention and our lives on things that will infect us. Mostly, they tempt us to become more self-centered. But there is a place that is a refuge from this darkening storm, a place where none of that is allowed to go.

The temple is like the area marked on the map—it's simply a location. Entering with a thorn on you isn't going to change the physical location or make it disappear. But there's a spirit that resides at the temple too—a feeling that permeates the place simply because of the things that are *not there*. If you carry the darkness with you, you'll destroy the essence of the refuge by entering it. But by becoming worthy before you enter—by removing the darkness and thorns from yourself—you put yourself in harmony with the place, so you can enter it without changing its nature. Even more, you can now enter the place and benefit from its unique attributes.

7. THE INTERVIEW

To show you're qualified to enter the temple, you have to meet with your bishop and then your stake president. In the interviews, they'll ask you a series of questions. I won't go through each of them, but here's an idea of what to expect:

- Do you have faith in God the Father, in his son Jesus Christ, and in the Holy Ghost? Do you believe in Christ's power to save (that is, do you understand the purpose and power of his Atonement)?
- Do you have a testimony of the restored gospel and are you willing to follow the man appointed today as God's living prophet, the modern Peter, and the only one who holds the keys of the kingdom of heaven? Do you avoid any groups that undermine or oppose Christ's church? And do you support your fellow Christians by attending meetings and serving there?
- Are you a responsible, caring, and loving family member?
- Are you honest? Are you chaste? Do you pay your tithing? Do you keep yourself free of harmful substances?

- In short, do you live the covenants you've made as a member of Christ's church and try your best to represent him?

You ought to go through these questions one by one and consider how you would answer them—being honest with yourself. That's a big deal, by the way—being honest with yourself. If you feel uncomfortable with any of these, that's okay. It's good to be introspective, and knowing where you fall short helps you to improve, till you really do qualify to enter the Lord's house.

After all this talk of worthiness and sacredness, remember you don't have to be perfect to enter the temple. After all, none of us are. Not yet—not as mortals. You have to meet the standards outlined by these interview questions—and that does mean becoming purified from quite a bit of darkness. Luckily, it's something we do with Christ's strength, not our own. And once we've crossed that threshold, meeting a certain level of worthiness, the temple helps us to keep getting better.

8. Confess and Forsake

It may be that you've done some things you shouldn't have, which you've never resolved. If it's weighing on your mind, speaking with the bishop is the Lord's way to fix that. It takes courage—usually the things that keep nagging your conscience are the very things you don't normally tell people. But confession is an important part of repenting and changing. Admitting your shortcomings to someone else—particularly to someone who's been called as a shepherd—helps you to be more perfectly honest with yourself and with the Lord. It was the Lord, after all, who recommended that we do this. And as we do, there's healing.

Jesus himself said, "I, the Lord, forgive sins, and am merciful unto those who confess their sins with humble hearts" (D&C 61:2). It may be hard—maybe the toughest thing you've ever done—but you'll be better off in the end. If these things are serious, it may take several months or more to resolve them fully. But eventually you'll be prepared and the bishop will recommend that you're worthy to enter the temple—and he'll sign a certificate as physical evidence of that.

More importantly, you'll have made yourself qualified—that is, you'll be the judge, and *you'll* know you're ready to enter. You'll then get to sign that certificate too, the temple recommend, as a physical way of showing the state of your soul.

9. FIRST PRINCIPLES AND ORDINANCES

You started preparing to be worthy for the temple when you were pretty young—eight years old—right about the time you memorized the fourth article of faith:

> We believe that the first principles and ordinances of the gospel are: first, faith in the Lord Jesus Christ; second, repentance; third, baptism by immersion for the remission of sins; fourth, laying on of hands for the gift of the Holy Ghost.

You'll study each of these in depth on your mission.

In fact (here's another side note), you'll spend a couple hours studying every morning for two years. Two hours isn't much. But 2 x 365 x 2 really adds up. I never realized how valuable that study time would be and what kind of a gospel scholar I might become by making good use of it. (You're thinking, "How much is there to know about dipping someone in water?" I thought that too–thought I knew about all there was to know about baptism. Boy was I wrong.) The study time is something you should look forward to. And it's not a bad idea to start following those patterns now. Maybe start with something small, like 10 minutes per day—something easy to achieve. Like I mentioned, a drip-by-drip strategy, something small and consistent (i.e., slow and steady), is much more valuable than hauling a couple five-gallon buckets and then forgetting about it. Establishing consistency with something simple will eventually create a habit.

So where were we? Oh yeah, we were making our way through the first principles and ordinances of the gospel: You have exercised faith in Christ—which means you believe in what people, including the prophets, have taught you about Christ and his power to save. You've at least believed it enough to want to change—that's repentance—and you've tried to be a better person because of it. When you were eight, you made a promise to be a Christian—that's what baptism was about. And God made a promise back—Dad put his hands on your head and confirmed you a member of Christ's band of soldiers and told you to receive the Holy Ghost. And because Dad holds the priesthood—God's authority delegated to man—you received that gift, which is the promise to have God's influence inside you, in your heart and mind.

All of these prepared you for the temple. They put a dotted line on the map of your life. In the small things at least, and maybe in the large things too, they guided you toward light and steered you away from darkness—a key part of getting ready.

10. Soldiers of Christ

As you continue to follow the Holy Ghost, you'll do the things that keep him nearby. Things like praying every day, and fasting on occasion, and repenting when you know you've done something that isn't right.

Baptism and *receiving* the Holy Ghost are one-time events, but they're cycles that can be renewed daily, and they'll lead you to something bigger—not just events but a change in your person—a change in who you are.

This change can be seen in an archetype I really like—that of the Christian soldier. It inspires a lot of heroic emotions in me. One of my favorite hymns, "Hope of Israel," puts it like this:

> Strike for Zion; down with error;
> Flash the sword above the foe!
> Every stroke disarms a foeman;
> Every step we conquering go.
> Hope of Israel, rise in might
> With the sword of truth and right;
> Sound the warcry, "Watch and pray!"
> Vanquish every foe today.

"Flash the sword above the foe!" I love it. These are soldiers who fight on behalf of Christ. Their warcry is "watch and pray"—which to me means to be mindful, to pay attention, both physically (watch) and spiritually (pray). And the enemy? *Mistruth* ("Down with error").

We become these soldiers as we take upon us Christ's name and Spirit—putting on the armor of God (Ephesians 6:13) and becoming a disciple. It means you're his representative, or, even better, his son. But it's not simply a matter of how you act, though that's important too. It's who you are. It's inside of you—and deep.

This soldier acts in Christ's stead—he does the things Christ would do if he were there. This means following Christ: You've seen movies that depict the Crusader trains—the king or champion rides at the front of an army stretched along a highway, with banners streaming in the wind.

I have another favorite hymn (written in 1812 by Anglican Bishop Reginald Heber, and often set to the same tune as "The Minstrel Boy"), which draws on this same imagery. The lyrics talk first about Stephen the martyr, then Christ's original Apostles, then finally us saints—each following in Christ's army:

> The Son of God goes forth to war,
> A kingly crown to gain;
> <u>His blood-red banner streams afar</u>:
> Who follows in His train?
> <u>Who best can drink his cup of woe</u>,
> Triumphant over pain,
> Who patient bears his cross below,
> He follows in His train.

That martyr first, <u>whose eagle eye</u>
<u>Could pierce beyond the grave,</u>
Who saw his Master in the sky
And called on Him to save,
<u>Like Him</u>, with pardon on His tongue,
In midst of mortal pain,
<u>He prayed for them that did the wrong</u>.
Who follows in His train?

A glorious band, the chosen few
On whom the Spirit came,
<u>Twelve valiant saints</u>, their hope they knew
And mocked the cross and flame.
They <u>met the tyrant's brandished steel,</u>
<u>The lion's gory mane;</u>
<u>They bowed their heads, the death to feel</u>:
Who follows in their train?

<u>A noble army, men and boys,</u>
<u>The matron and the maid,</u>
Around the Savior's throne rejoice,
<u>In robes of light</u> arrayed.
<u>They climbed the steep ascent</u> of Heav'n,
Through peril, toil and pain;
O God, to us <u>may grace be given</u>,
To follow in their train.

The hymn asks us whether we're ready to follow Christ, Stephen, and the twelve—even when the path leads to torture and death. They each paid a high price to build the kingdom of heaven. As the hymn says, the ascent is steep. But the kingdom of heaven is worth far more than the cost of getting there. Thinking of these noble examples gives me courage to march forward, even into a terrible battle. It fills me with life and enthusiasm.

Enthusiasm is a pretty cool word too: It originally meant "to be inspired or possessed by a god"—meaning to have God within you. That literally happens when we receive the gift of the Holy Ghost—we have God inside our hearts. And that spirit changes us into these Christian soldiers who are willing to die in the service of others and of God.

Joseph Smith said it in a way that rivals the speeches of the most inspiring generals: "Shall we not go on in so great a cause?... Courage, brethren; and on, on to the victory!" (D&C 128:22).

11. TEMPLE JOURNAL

As another way to prepare, I recommend you keep a journal—a place where you record your spiritual thoughts. You can start by jotting down your insights as you read this book.

I may be a little biased, but I think writing is super important. Alma, Nephi, Moroni, and just about every other ancient prophet—they were writers. And we benefit from what they wrote. Maybe that's putting it too lightly. It's hard to describe the value of their writings. The point is that you will benefit from what you write, and so will your family and friends. It will help you hold on to what matters—those most important things that we mortals are so good at forgetting.

To give you an example, I've included a few entries from my own journal, dates and all:

Temple Tips | 19 Nov 2009

I started asking the old guys at the temple this question: "Do you have any tips for me on my temple study?" Here are some of their answers:

- "Let me think about it. Oh, I know. In the October *Ensign* there was an article about the home as a temple."
- "Read *The Old Testament.* A lot of the stuff is right in there, word for word."
- "Mm. No. Not really."
- "Look at The Book of Abraham."
- "You should ask one of the temple presidency that question."
- "Boyd K. Packer's book. And other ones like that. But be careful you're not reading ones that are opinion."
- "When Isaiah says *mysteries*, he's talking about the temple."
- "Just come." Pauses. Looks up at the ceiling. Looks at me again and nods, affirming that he has the right answer, and repeats: "Just come."

3 Nov 2010 | I did initiatory for Benjamin Robinson, born in 1707 in Shankill Parish, Dramore Dioce, Armagh, Ireland.

Temple and Tom | 24 Jun 2011

I just had dinner (at Red Iguana) with Tom. I told him how Meagan was a little freaked out when she went to the temple for the first time. A lot of people are like that though. Tom said it's because people usually think the gospel we get at church is the main event. So they're shocked to realize that the temple is the main thing, and the sacrament meetings were something leading up to, or strengthening us to keep, the ordinances and covenants of the temple. But the temple really is the main thing. It always was.

Again and Again | 5 Oct 2011

Seven times. Naaman had to dip seven times. And he wasn't healed on the sixth either. Sometimes it's a small thing, done repeatedly, and it's only in the repetition that something happens. (I learned this in *House of Glory* by S. Michael Wilcox.)

The Gate of Heaven | 12 Aug 2012

I taught Elders Quorum today about the temple. I asked them what was valuable about dressing in cap and gown and walking down an aisle. Then I asked how they'd justify having a temple ceremony to an atheist friend. Then I told the story of Jacob's Ladder and taught them about the circle-and-square symbol that represents the four corners of the earth uniting with the eternal heavens—the nexus where the two worlds meet.

Jon raised his hand and told an interesting story: Last  night, he was on the phone with his former co-worker who was drunk and demanding answers to "all that temple mumbo jumbo." Jon said, "I want you to tell me what you learned in all those war-strategy books you've been reading, and I want you to tell me right now." The man said he could give the gist of it, but that to really get it Jon would have to read them all himself. Jon told him the temple was the same way, that he'd never really understand until he had paid the price.

Axis Mundi | 14 Sep 2012

I went to a conference yesterday called The Temple on Mount Zion. I learned the term *axis mundi*:

> The *axis mundi* (also cosmic axis, world axis, world pillar, columna cerului, center of the world), in religion or mythology, is the world center and/or the connection between Heaven and Earth. As the celestial pole and geographic pole, it expresses a point of connection between sky and earth where the four compass directions meet. At this point, travel and correspondence happen between higher and lower realms. Communication from lower realms may ascend to higher ones and blessings from higher realms may descend to lower ones and be disseminated to all. The spot functions as the *omphalos* (navel), the world's point of beginning. (Wikipedia)

The temple, then, is the true axis mundi. Pretty cool.

I also learned the term *hierophany* (from Greek meaning "to reveal or bring to light the sacred or holy") and was reminded of the term *theophany* ("the appearance of a deity to a human; divine disclosure").

Brigham City Temple Dedication | 23 Sep 2012

President Packer was listing rooms and ordinances and he said, "and the holy of holies where other ordinances are performed."

12. WHY COVENANTS

I love naming things. In fact, I often come up with the title to a story before I think of the story itself. On my mission, I even started a project to name every chapter in *The Book of Mormon*. That's why I like the way Victor Ludlow, a BYU professor and expert on Isaiah, gave names to the five main covenants of salvation:

Baptism: The Gateway
Sacrament: The Renewal
Priesthood: The Service
Endowment: The Gift
Sealing: The Bond

As you know, the temple is about making these last two covenants (which have specific promises embedded in them). To a modern mind, covenants can seem a little strange, so let's talk more about them and why they're important (relying heavily on what I learned from Dr. Ludlow).

First, covenants teach us *what to do*—they're the path that leads us to "live after the manner of happiness," as Nephi said (2 Nephi 5:27). In other words, they're Heavenly Father's way of saying, "If you want to be happy, do these things." For example, the sacrament tells us to call ourselves Christians and to remember Christ at all times. Following the covenants sanctifies us, through our actions (faith) and through the Spirit (grace).

Second, covenants give us *motivations*: After he tells us what to do, God explains the rewards for doing it. Going back to the sacrament—it promises we'll have his Spirit as a guide—that's the reward. Covenants also warn us about the natural consequences of *not* listening to God's guidelines—something like this: "I'm not trying to be mean, but if you play in the street, you could get hit by a car." Understanding consequences motivates us to be stronger than the temptations that pull on us.

Third, covenants are *gateways*—they're physical rites that show what we've accomplished and what's ahead, sort of like a mile marker on the freeway or receiving a diploma in a graduation ceremony. With diplomas, you don't really need the physical piece of paper to get a job, but it's a symbol of the skills and knowledge that *are* necessary. The thing itself wouldn't mean a thing if it weren't for the fact that it represents so much. The rites show that you're qualified (what's in the past) for divine blessings (what's in the future). These gateways allow us to measure our progress on the Lord's map.

Alma the elder, while talking with a group of future saints at the waters of Mormon, turned these into a rhetorical question:

> If this be the desire of your hearts, what have you against being baptized in the name of the Lord, <u>as a witness</u> before him <u>that ye have entered into a covenant</u> with him, <u>that ye will serve</u> him and keep his commandments, <u>that he may pour out his Spirit</u> more abundantly upon you? (Mosiah 18:10)

You'll notice that he lists both our part (to serve) and the Lord's part (to pour out his Spirit)—and we enter into this contract through the rite of baptism. The sacrament, which essentially renews the same covenant, uses similar language: "That they may *witness* unto thee..."

This concept of *witnessing* reminds me of another story—if you'll indulge me for a bit. What we now call Texas was territory that belonged to the Mexican government after their revolution to overthrow the Spanish. But the population of Texas was mostly Americans, so there was a dispute over who should govern it. War broke out, which led to a band of only about 200 rough, American soldiers holing up in an old Spanish mission called the Alamo. Legend says that, when the time came to fight or flee, Colonel William Travis took his sabre and drew a line in the sand. Then he asked those men who'd stand with him, who were willing to fight against impossible odds—he asked them to show it by stepping over that line. Only one man fell out of ranks that day.

Here's why I think that's interesting: Whether a man steps over a line or not doesn't really matter. That is, not unless it's linked to an inner state of mind. That day, by taking that step, they showed what kind of men they were on the inside. They witnessed with their bodies that they were committed in their hearts. It moved the decision from the immaterial world into the physical universe around them—it *real*-ized the choice.

We're given that same gift and privilege every week at the sacrament table. We step across a line, so to speak, by picking up the bread. And we show externally, to our fellow saints and even to the world, that we're indeed followers of Jesus the anointed—our Savior, Priest, and King.

Every ordinance is like that—it's a line in the sand that we're invited to cross in order to show (or witness) on the outside what we're like on the inside.

13. SYMBOLISM

As you know, I received a degree not long ago, and I learned a couple of things going through the ritual—things I thought I'd mention to you.

In the ceremony, you start with the tassel on the left, and when you commence, the tassel moves to the right—symbolizing the progression from *student* to *graduate*. You also wear specific clothing. (I wore a long, white hood, symbolizing an English degree; my cloak was black with long, closed sleeves, which represented a master's degree.) You also wear a cap, which should be worn a certain way—flat on top, like a crown (it's disrespectful to let it slouch).

When you think about some of this stuff, it seems a little silly. All in all, there's no practical purpose for any of the graduation ceremony—at least if you don't believe in the symbolism of the ritual. Without the symbolism, there's no reason left to do it.

THE CAP

The cap should be worn so that the mortarboard is level. It should not be cocked to the back or side of the head. The crown should be approximately one inch above the eyebrows. The front of the cap is indicated on the inside of the crown. Men remove their caps during the playing of the National Anthem and the School song.

the School song.

THE TASSEL

Tassels are worn over the left or right temple. All graduates should wear the tassel on the same side *for uniformity*. Some schools switch the tassel from left to right - in unison - after all diplomas are received.

THE GOWN

The gown should be removed from the

John A. Widtsoe, a modern apostle, taught,

We live in a world of symbols. We know nothing, except by symbols. We make a few marks on a sheet of paper, and we say that they form a word, which stands for love, or hate, or charity, or God, or eternity. The marks may not be very beautiful to the eye. No one finds fault with the symbols on the pages of a book because they are not as mighty in their own beauty as the things which they represent. We do not quarrel with the symbol G-O-D because it is not very beautiful, yet represents the majesty of God. We are glad to have symbols, if only the meaning of the symbols is brought home to us... No man or woman can come out of the temple endowed as he should be, unless he has seen, beyond the symbol, the mighty realities for which the symbols stand. ("Temple Worship")

Symbols are essential to understanding just about anything. They're particularly important in the temple. Having said that, I'll share something that Sioux pointed out to me:

To avoid idolatry, Islam forbids making any sort of image of God. Ancient Catholicism was basically the opposite: Holy relics were seen as having power in themselves, not just in what they represented (like the True Cross that Saladin captured from the Crusaders before he retook Jerusalem). These two could be thought of as extremes on the ends of a spectrum: One side condemns the symbols; the other holds them so high they block the view of the real thing.

A symbol should be a pathway to something higher—something that illuminates. If it makes things clearer, then it's doing its job (and you're doing yours). But it should never become a destination in itself.

14. Personal Study

Scripture

- Abraham 1 (Focus on verses 2-4, 18-19, and 31. Also, verse 26 has an interesting clue about how ancient Egyptian temples mimicked our temple ceremonies—something Hugh Nibley wrote about.)

Sermon

- "The Holy Temple," an official pamphlet from the church

Book

- *The Holy Temple* by Boyd K. Packer

Go to jwashburn.com/books/dearjeff for links to these readings and a complete bibliography.

Initiatory

And thou shalt bring Aaron and his sons unto the door of the tabernacle of the congregation, and wash them with water. And thou shalt put upon Aaron the holy garments, and anoint him, and sanctify him.

— *Exodus 40:12-13*

15. Initiation

Initiatory is an interesting concept. People get initiated into gangs, college fraternities, even the Masons and military groups. The idea is very simple—it's the starting point, where you go from being outside of a circle to being on the inside. That's a bad thing if you're getting into a gang. But it's a good thing if you're joining a group devoted to doing what Christ did when he was walking around down here.

Some people criticize the church by calling it a cult. Let's look at the word *cult* for a second (remember, don't panic). Here's what Google told me:

> *cult* /kəlt/ Noun. (1) A system of religious veneration and devotion directed toward a particular object or figure. (2) A relatively small group of people having religious beliefs or practices regarded by others as strange or sinister.

We Mormons venerate and devote ourselves to Christ, religiously, so that means we fit definition one. We're also a relatively small group, and the number of us who have made and keep temple promises is even smaller. And some people, since they haven't read this book yet, assume (based on what they *don't* know) that we're strange. So we also fit definition two. But usually when people call us a cult, they're thinking of something creepy and sinister like you'd read about in a Dan Brown novel. These are voices from the outside—who don't follow the precepts and so don't understand them. And their perspective couldn't be further from the truth.

By entering the temple, you're joining a small group of

Christ's followers—it's as simple as that. As one proof, I'd like to offer this: The temple ceremony is a progression, an upward journey toward the celestial room—a room designed to represent the highest heaven. In the Provo temple, a massive picture of Christ hangs on the wall, dominating the celestial room. It shows Christ at his second coming, standing on a cloud with his arms outstretched—still inviting people to come unto him. He welcomes those who complete the ceremony. So if it's a cult, it's the cult of Christ. Better, perhaps, to think of it as the soldiers of Christ like we talked about—those who follow in his train. It's a brotherhood and a sisterhood, a family circle that connects us, as Christ said, "And the glory which thou gavest me I have given them; that they may be one, even as we are one" (John 17:22).

The initiatory is simply the first step in entering that circle.

16. INITIATORY

I want you to go back to the beginning of this chapter and re-read that opening epigraph (Exodus 40:12-13), which talks about five specific actions. Do you know what each of them are? (If someone asked you what they meant, how would you explain?)

The initiatory is the first of three parts of the temple ceremony (it's followed by the endowment and the sealing). President Packer wrote,

> The ordinances of <u>washing and anointing</u> are referred to often in the temple as <u>initiatory ordinances</u>... [which

are] mostly symbolic in nature, but [promise] definite, immediate blessings as well as future blessings... You will be <u>officially clothed in the garment</u> and promised marvelous blessings in connection with it. It is important that you listen carefully as these ordinances are administered and that you try to remember the blessings promised and the conditions upon which they will be realized. ("The Holy Temple" pamphlet)

You'll notice strong similarities as you compare this chapter's epigraph with President Packer's quote above. Our modern temple initiatory is basically a streamlined version of an ancient ceremony. (This is also the case with the endowment—while some details have been updated, the core is the same.)

The early latter-day saints had something called "the school of the prophets" which included a kind of forerunner to our current temple ceremony. They were instructed on how to initiate:

Ye shall not receive any among you into this school save he is clean from the blood of this generation; and he shall be received by the ordinance of the washing of feet, for unto this end was the ordinance of the washing of feet instituted. (D&C 88:138-139)

So only a certain type of person was admitted—specifically a person who had been cleansed of sin. Again, I feel like I ought to emphasize that this isn't saying, "Keep out the people with thorns." It's saying, "Bring everyone in, even the people who have thorns—just make sure to purify them first."

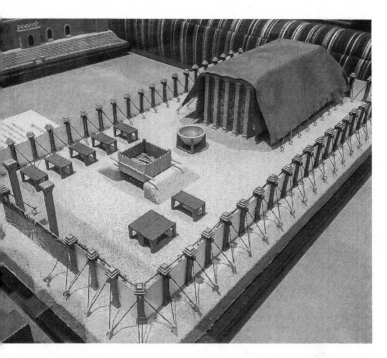

Also, the Lord calls the washing of feet an ordinance. It's not the exact same thing as the temple initiatory, but there are some strong similarities. As the Lord concluded teaching Joseph in section 88, he said to do the ordinance of washing feet "according to the pattern given in the thirteenth chapter of John's testimony concerning me" (D&C 88:141). So he was basically saying, "I officiated this ordinance while I was on earth; go read what John wrote about how I did it." And if you follow that instruction, you'll read that the Lord, before he started that ordinance, "laid aside his garments; and took a towel, and girded himself" (John 13:4). He then washed them before pronouncing, "Ye are clean, but not all" (John 13:10). That's the ordinance.

The Lord told the latter-day apostles to attain a similar

blessing—that if they wanted to receive great promises they should meet a certain standard: "Behold how great is your calling. Cleanse your hearts and your garments, lest the blood of this generation be required at your hands" (D&C 112:33). This instruction applies to you and me just as it did to them, and it's central to initiatory.

17. Washing and Anointing

The symbolism of washing is pretty straightforward. I don't mean to downplay it—it's definitely worth pondering, but you're already familiar because of baptism: It's about cleansing. And it's about what's in the past—it's looking backward.

Anointing is not quite so obvious, so we're going to dig deeper.

In ancient times, kings and priests were the highest ranks in society—King Mosiah and Priest Alma are a good example; you see the pattern throughout the Bible too. These were the greatest titles a mortal could receive, and to be given either of them you had to be anointed. Basically, anointing is a priesthood ordinance that involves the pouring of sacred oil from a horn onto the initiate.

In *The Old Testament*, kings to be—that is, boys whose destiny it was to become a king—were anointed to that position. One of the most memorable instances of this is when David was anointed as a boy:

> Then Samuel took the horn of oil, and anointed him in the midst of his brethren: and the Spirit of the

Lord came upon David from that day forward. (1 Samuel 16:13)

But when David was anointed at that moment, he didn't become king immediately. Instead, his anointing affirmed his *future* calling—he was anointed *to become* king. Later, in 2 Samuel 2:4, he was anointed king—the actual thing this time. So an anointing can be looking forward to a future event, or it can be the event itself.

The picture below shows an Egyptian king being anointed, which is another example of the second kind of anointing (from the *Jewish Encyclopedia*). Incidentally, in his hand the king holds an *ankh*, a symbol representing eternal life.

The word *Christ* has roots in the Greek word *khristos*, which means "the anointed." *Khristos* is a translation of the Hebrew word *mashiah*, or, as we say in English, *messiah*—which also means "the one who was anointed." Peter taught us that Christ was "foreordained before the foundation of the world" (1 Peter 1:20)—in other words, he was anointed to his calling ahead of time. John the Revelator said Christ was "the Lamb slain from the foundation of the world" (Revelation 13:8). God the Father testified of his son's anointing, saying he was "my Beloved and Chosen from the beginning, [who] said unto me—Father, thy will be done, and the glory be thine forever" (Moses 4:2). Christ also testified of his own pre-appointed destiny when he spoke to the brother of Jared:

> I am he who was prepared from the foundation of the world to redeem my people. Behold, I am Jesus Christ. I am the Father and the Son. In me shall all mankind have life, and that eternally, even they who shall believe on my name; and they shall become my sons and my daughters. (Ether 3:14)

This scripture is especially cool because it looks forward in two ways: It mentions Christ's anointing looking forward to what he *would* do; then it also looks forward to what's in store for us mortals: "They shall become my sons and daughters." In other words, we'll eventually inherit Christ's perfection as his spiritual offspring (see Mosiah 5:7). Perhaps when that promise is fulfilled, it will be a ceremony confirmed with oil too.

Now, one final example: You're not a Melchizedek Priesthood holder yet, but when you become one you'll have the chance to administer to the sick. The church's *Handbook 2* explains that it takes two priesthood holders: The first pours the oil, then puts his hands on the person's head (just like the Savior did, I might add), and says the words of anointing. Then with both priesthood holders putting their hands on the person's head, the second priesthood holder *seals* the anointing and adds a blessing (see 20.6.2-3). This seems to match up with the immediate type of anointing, where you actually become king, or, in this case, where you actually become healed. But it might also be the kind that looks forward to healing (it happens, as they say, on the Lord's timetable and not our own).

So to sum up, washing purifies the past, and anointing promises the future. Anointing looks forward. And just as Christ was anointed for his great mission long before it ever happened, we can be anointed looking forward to our destinies, as his children and his heirs. This is the purpose of the initiatory ordinance.

18. Kings and Priests

Now you have an idea of the purpose of an anointing. And you've seen that it applies to earthly kings as well as heavenly ones. As I mentioned, it also applies to priests.

The Lord gave detailed steps to Moses and Aaron on how to anoint a priest. The purpose was to purify the priest and make him holy:

- **Exodus 40:9** "And thou shalt take the anointing oil, and anoint the tabernacle, and all that is therein, and shalt hallow it, and all the vessels thereof: and it shall be holy." (So this anointing made these things holy—it set them apart as special and separate from ordinary use.)

- **Exodus 40:15** "And thou shalt anoint them, as thou didst anoint their father, that they may minister unto me in the priest's office: for their anointing shall surely be an everlasting priesthood throughout their generations." (This hints at the point of anointing—it's aimed at an everlasting priesthood.)
- **Exodus 40:16** "According to all that the Lord commanded him, so did he." (It repeats seven times that Moses did as the "Lord commanded"—seven, which could represent perfection, showing that Moses was exact in obeying the commandments of God—in setting things apart as holy.)
- **Exodus 19:5-6** "If ye will obey my voice indeed, and keep my covenant, then ye shall be a peculiar treasure unto me above all people: for all the earth is mine. And ye shall be unto me <u>a kingdom of priests and an holy nation</u>." (The concept of a kingdom of priests is fascinating. It ties the ideas of *king* and *priest* into one—a *kingdom* is the domain of a king, and a *priest* is a religious leader—making a holy nation.)

The *Old Testament Student Manual* has some helpful commentary on this, based on 1 Samuel 10:1. It discusses why Saul's anointing ordinance was significant:

Anointing with oil in priesthood service is as old as Adam. And, since the Lord set up the kingdom of Israel and revealed the laws that were to govern their kings, it was altogether fitting that these kings be anointed with oil. "Anointing with oil was <u>a symbol of endowment with the Spirit of God</u>; as the oil itself, by virtue of the strength which it gives to the vital spirits, was a symbol of the Spirit of God as the principle of divine and spiritual power... When Saul was consecrated as king by anointing, the monarchy was inaugurated as <u>a divine institution</u>, through which henceforth the Lord would also... <u>bestow upon His people the gifts of His Spirit for the building up of His kingdom</u>. As the priests were consecrated by anointing to be the media of the ethical blessings of divine grace for Israel, so the king was consecrated by anointing to be <u>the vehicle and medium of all the blessings of grace</u> which the Lord, as the God-king, would confer upon His people through the institution of a civil government. Through this anointing, which was performed by Samuel under the direction of God, the king was set apart from the rest of the nation as 'anointed of the Lord.'" But Samuel anointed Saul to be "captain" even though he was later called king. This title should have served as a reminder that the Lord was still king.

I won't summarize that because I think you can put those pieces together—to see the significance of being anointed as king or priest. By the way, this is as good a time as any to admit a dilemma: On one hand, I want to be explicit and direct as I try to guide you through this material. But I don't want to give you the idea that the study and thinking are all *my* job. I hope you'll take it on yourself to put things together once I've handed the pieces over. And I'm sure you'll find new pieces on your own too, which I hope you'll let me in on—I still have a lot to learn too.

Okay, let's take it from here back to Christ—after all, he

was the paradigm of these high offices. Hebrews calls Christ "an high priest of good things to come" (Hebrews 9:11) and "a merciful and faithful high priest in things pertaining to God, to make reconciliation for the sins of the people" (Hebrews 2:17). David poetically said Christ was "a priest for ever after the order of Melchizedek" (Psalm 110:4).

Christ was king too, "King of all the earth" (Psalm 47:7). When Pilate asked him if he was King of the Jews, he answered, "[I am, even as] thou sayest" (JST Mark 15:4). But he didn't claim an earthly domain. He said, "My kingdom is not of this world: if my kingdom were of this world, then would my servants fight, that I should not be delivered to the Jews" (John 18:36). He later described his heavenly throne: "Hereafter shall ye see the Son of man sitting on the right hand of power, and coming in the clouds of heaven" (Matt 26:64)—the same image we see in that painting in the Provo temple. In the hymn "I Know that My Redeemer Lives," he's called "my prophet, priest, and king."

So Christ is *the* King and *the* Priest. And we're his spiritual sons and daughters—we're born a second time through his Atonement—he purifies our sinful selves so we can become new people. "And if children, then heirs; heirs of God, and joint-heirs with Christ; if it so be that we suffer with him, that we may be also glorified together" (Romans 8:17). So we will be with him—kings to *the* King, and priests to *the* Priest.

Doctrine and Covenants 76 is all about the inheritances that God has laid out for his children (definitely one to study thoroughly). In verses 55-56, it talks about the people who will inherit the highest glory: "They are they into whose hands the Father has given all things—they are they who are <u>priests</u> and <u>kings</u>, who have received of his fulness, and of his glory."

John the Revelator taught this same idea, that the saints of God would eventually receive such a high and holy office: "[Christ] hath made us kings and priests unto God and his Father; to him be glory and dominion for ever and ever. Amen" (Revelation 1:6).

These are the promises God makes to us in the temple covenants.

This is what we're being initiated into.

19. HOLY GARMENTS

Now let's talk about garments. You've probably heard Mom and Dad use that word here and there. The word *garment* is a generic term that means about the same thing as *clothing*. A T-shirt is a garment. Your favorite jeans are too. But the temple garments are holy—meaning they're set apart as a special thing, in their own distinct category. We call temple garments "garments," but we really ought to be more respectful. The proper name would be "holy garments" or "sacred clothing," because they're something God has asked his servants to wear—this he "revealed to the Prophet Joseph Smith when the endowment ceremony was given to him" ("The Holy Temple").

> The ancient priests also put on special clothing symbolic of the Lord's covenants with Israel. Today, symbolic of our transformation into "new creatures in Christ," we put on sacred clothing, a new garment, after the initiatory washing and anointing ordinances.

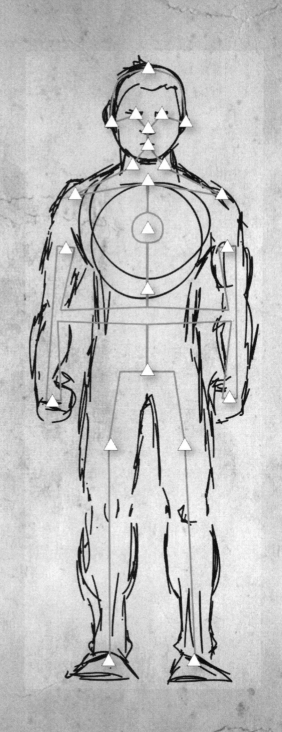

<u>We wear this special white underclothing afterward throughout our lives as a reminder of our covenants and as protection through our close association with the Holy Spirit</u>. Since the initiatory ordinances prepare us to become truly begotten sons and daughters of Christ, we begin to assume a new spiritual identity, symbolized with a new name, before proceeding to the endowment session itself. (Victor Ludlow, *Principles and Practices of the Restored Gospel*)

So when you're initiated as a warrior of Christ, you commit to wearing this holy uniform as a way to remember who you are. I'd like to highlight three points President Packer taught in relation to this holy temple garment:

- It's a reminder that "represents sacred covenants."
- As it covers the body, "it fosters modesty."
- And it "becomes a shield and protection to the wearer."

Some people think that the temple garment will restrict their wardrobe, but President Packer said, "Only clothing that is immodest or extreme in style would be incompatible with wearing the garment. Any member of the Church, whether he or she has been to the temple or not, would in proper spirit want to avoid extreme or revealing fashions." And then he told this awesome story that teaches part of the reason behind the temple garment:

> [Once] one of the brethren was invited to speak to... the Navy Chaplains Training School in Newport, Rhode Island. The audience included a number of high-ranking naval chaplains from the Catholic, Protestant, and Jewish faiths. In the question-and-answer period one

of the chaplains asked, "Can you tell us something about the special underwear that some Mormon servicemen wear?" The implication was, "Why do you do that? Isn't it strange? Doesn't that present a problem?" [The brother] responded with a question...: "In civilian life and also when conducting the meetings in the military service you wear clerical clothing, do you not?" The chaplain said he did... "I would suppose that that has some importance to you, that in a sense it sets you apart from the rest of your congregation. It is your uniform, as it were, of the ministry... It reminds you of who you are and what your obligations and covenants are. It is a continual reminder that you are a member of the clergy, that you regard yourself as a servant of the Lord, and that you are responsible to live in such a way as to be worthy of your ordination... A major difference between your churches and ours is that we do not have a professional clergy, as you do. The congregations are all presided over by local leaders... men called from all walks of life. Yet they are ordained to the priesthood... They are set apart to presiding positions as presidents, counselors, and leaders in various categories. The women, too, share in that responsibility and in those obligations. The man who heads our congregation on Sunday as the bishop may go to work on Monday as a postal clerk, as an office worker, a farmer, a doctor; or he may be an air-force pilot or a naval officer. By our standard he is as much an ordained minister as you are by your standard. He is recognized as such by most governments. We draw something of the same benefits from this special clothing as you would draw from your clerical vestments. The difference is that <u>we wear ours under our clothing instead of outside, for we are employed in various occupations in addition to our service in the Church</u>. These sacred things we do not wish to parade before the world."

That brother went on to explain to them that the temple garments have a deeper meaning too—that they symbolically remind us of the temple covenants. And he told them he wasn't going to discuss these specifically, "not that they are secret, but because they are sacred." He did explain, though, that "the garment, covering the body, is a visual and tactile reminder of these covenants. For many Church members the garment has <u>formed a barrier of protection</u> when the wearer has been faced with temptation. Among other things it symbolizes our deep respect for the laws of God."

Paul used an interesting phrase when writing to the Galatians: "For as many of you as have been baptized into Christ <u>have put on Christ</u>" (Galatians 3:27). What exactly does it mean to *put on* Christ? When I put something on (clothing is the only thing I can think of), I'm covering myself and creating a new appearance. To put on Christ could then mean to cover what I used to be with a new me—a *me* that appears like Christ. The temple garments symbolize this metaphor of putting on Christ.

The initiatory is focused on the physical body, linking the body to its spiritual purpose. Our religion glorifies the body more than most other Christians. We believe there was a reason that Christ, after dying, came back to

TEMPORAL MATTERS: GARMENTS

President Packer said this about the logistics: "Garments are provided by an agency of the Church—and are generally available to members throughout the world through a distribution program operated by the Church."

You can order them online at http://store.lds.org/.

I recommend the scoop-neck tops (it's not cool to wear crew necks underneath right now, but I'm sure the trend will swing back soon). I also recommend polyester—they're durable and dry quickly. I prefer them a little snug (better than too loose), but that's up to you. And my last tip: get the "tall" version for your tops—which means the torso is a little longer and stays tucked in better.

his physical body. We also believe that when God raises up his children in the hereafter, he will do it by making their bodies, as well as their souls, glorious. In that way, our bodies and souls are connected at a fundamental level, even now in mortality. As Isaiah put it, and I think it's fair to say he's talking about eternal beings here, "They that wait upon the Lord shall renew their strength; they shall mount up with wings as eagles; they shall run, and not be weary; and they shall walk, and not faint" (Isaiah 40:31, see also D&C 89:20).

There's one more thing I want to say about the symbolism of the garment. In the writings of Zechariah, the second to last book of *The Old Testament*, we read a cool story about holy garments:

> Now Joshua was clothed with filthy garments, and stood before the angel. And [the angel] answered and spake unto those that stood before him, saying, "Take away the filthy garments from him." And unto [Joshua] he said, "Behold, I have caused thine iniquity to pass from thee, and I will clothe thee with <u>change of raiment</u>..." So they set <u>a fair mitre upon his head, and clothed him with garments</u>. And the angel of the Lord stood by... saying, "Thus saith the Lord of hosts: if thou wilt walk in my ways, and if thou wilt keep my charge, then thou shalt also judge my house, and shalt also keep my courts, and I will give thee places to walk among these that stand by." (Zechariah 3:3-7)

Mitre is a word you're probably not familiar with. It's a type of ceremonial headgear—basically a crown. So Joshua's clothing was dirty, and the angel gave him new clean clothing along with the crown and the office that went with it. Going back to our discussion of symbolism, our literal clothing doesn't matter too much, not alone. But what it represents *is* important—and in this case, clean and holy garments represent the state of that person's heart and might—body and soul. As the letter to the Ephesians says,

> Stand therefore, having your loins girt about with truth, and having on the breastplate of righteousness; and your feet shod with the preparation of the gospel of peace; above all, taking the shield of faith, wherewith ye shall be able to quench all the fiery darts of the wicked. And take the helmet of salvation, and the sword of the Spirit, which is the word of God: praying

always with all prayer and supplication in the Spirit, and watching thereunto with all perseverance and supplication for all saints. (Ephesians 6:14-18)

You can see the Christian soldier in your mind, thanks to this poetic verse. And you may have noticed that the armor covers every part of the body, from his helmet of salvation down to his hobnailed boots.

It's an honor to wear the garment—an ever-present reminder whose soldiers we are and what it is we're fighting for. And I hope it's a privilege you look forward to.

20. The Spiritual Timeline

It takes a bit of daring to share a scripture from Isaiah, but here goes:

Let them bring them forth, and show us what shall happen: let them show the former things, what they be, that we may consider them, and know the latter end of them; or declare us things for to come. Show the things that are to come hereafter, that we may know that ye are gods. (Isaiah 41:22-23)

Nephi said, "The words of Isaiah are not plain unto you, nevertheless they are plain unto all those that are filled with the spirit of prophecy" (2 Nephi 6:5). I can't claim to understand Isaiah yet, but I'm learning (after all, the Lord himself said in 3 Nephi 23:1, "A commandment I give unto you that ye search these things diligently; for great are the words of Isaiah"). For now, I just want to point out how this scripture distinguishes the three main parts of our spiritual timeline: (1) "the former things"—that is, whatever came before; (2) we can insert *now* as the middle part, or borrow "preparatory state" from Alma; and (3) "the things that are to come hereafter."

This ties back to the ordinances: Some are about purifying past shortcomings. Some are promises for the hereafter, when the mortal machine stops working because the eternal one has taken its place. And some promises are for right now—our mortal, immediate future—to assist us in keeping the covenants, and to help us follow God's path in this preparatory state. In his intercessory prayer, Christ said, "I have glorified thee [Father] on the earth: I have finished the work which thou gavest me to do" (John 17:4). And like Christ, you, Jeff, have a particular work you're supposed to accomplish while you're alive. And so do we all.

This segmentation of past, present, and future is something you ought to listen for as you're going through the temple, particularly during the initiatory.

21. CHOOSE YOUR OWN ADVENTURE

I mentioned earlier how we're soldiers up against the powers of darkness. A real battle rages on, and the ground we're fighting over is heart and mind.

A war makes you think of bad guys, and I want to quickly mention something: Even the worst people who ever lived aren't bad guys in the eternal scheme. I know that's weird to think, but it's true. They're just as much children of God as you and I. To back that up, Christ taught us, "Love your enemies, bless them that curse you, do good to them that hate you, and pray for them which despitefully use you, and persecute you," (Matthew 5:44). He also said, "Inasmuch as ye have done it unto one of the least of these my brethren, ye have done it unto me" (Matthew 25:40). I think he wanted us to remember that those people—those who hate and despise and persecute—are still our brothers and sisters.

I bring this up so I can point out the real enemy. Nephi was the type of hero that comes to mind when you think of "good guys." Well, in the chapter some call "the psalm of Nephi," he said this, speaking poetically to his own heart: "No longer droop in sin. Rejoice, O my heart, and give place no more for the enemy of my soul" (2 Nephi 4:28). In other words, Nephi, the exemplary hero, admitted that the enemy of his soul was in his heart—he'd actually made some room for it in there. This shows that the enemy isn't any specific individual—they're all children of God. But the enemy is inside every individual. It lives in our hearts. It's sin. It's imperfection. It's mistruth.

If you look only at that aspect, things can look pretty bleak:

> For all flesh is corrupted before me; and the powers of darkness prevail upon the earth, among the children of men, in the presence of all the hosts of heaven. (D&C 38:11)

The good news, though, is that God has made a way for the good guys to win. And that way is Christ (he called himself "the way," in fact). Christ will eventually conquer that enemy in our hearts—he'll change our personalities till that's no longer part of us. And he offers this healing to everyone—the grace of God. To not just partially but fully

THOU SHALT LOVE THY GOD

With all thy soul

AND THY NEIGHBOR

AS THYSELF.

— St. Matthew 22:37–39

access that grace, we have to trust him and follow what he taught—to prepare for the hereafter. Alma put it this way:

> Therefore, as they had become carnal, sensual, and devilish, by nature, this probationary state became a state for them to prepare; it became a preparatory state. (Alma 42:10)

I like that Alma calls it "a preparatory state." Usually when you're preparing something, it means the main event is still about to come. And that's definitely the case with us. This life can be pretty fantastic at times. But even at its best, it's just a shadow of what God has coming:

> Eye hath not seen, nor ear heard, neither have entered into the heart of man, the things which God hath prepared for them that love him. (1 Corinthians 2:9)

That's a pretty hefty promise.

Notice, too, that "for them that love him" is a qualifier:

TEMPORAL MATTERS: REPETITION

I'm telling you this stuff so your first time at the temple will be a good experience—because it ought to be.

But some of it still won't make complete sense right now. Fortunately, you're going to go again and again. And as you go, just like Naaman, the repetition will build it into a fuller and fuller experience. You'll learn more each time, and you'll understand things the 20th time that you didn't understand the 10th. And so on into the hundreds, maybe thousands.

It limits the search results, you might say—so there's some exclusivity to what he's talking about. Loving God is the first commandment. And Paul's saying that if you keep that, you're in. Christ also taught, "If ye love me, keep my commandments" (John 14:15). So if we really love him, the natural fruit of that love is to do what he taught—because we know that really will make us and everyone else most happy.

So we're left with that choice—will we love God and do what he says? Or will we choose to love ourselves more? Better yet, do we listen to the enemy in our hearts that teaches us to be selfish, or do we listen to the Spirit that whispers to be self*less*?

And that's where temple covenants come in.

Covenants are promises we make about walking a certain path. And that path, God promises, will lead us to a reward. So each of God's promises rests on us, in a way:

> All victory and glory is brought to pass unto you through your diligence, faithfulness, and prayers of faith. (D&C 103:36)

In other words, God has great rewards he wants to give us, but receiving them rests on our own choices—whether we're going to be faithful to him. Read over that verse again: God is the one who brings the victory and glory, by his grace, but he brings it through our faithfulness. C. S. Lewis put it this way: "After all, you must have a capacity to receive, or even omnipotence can't give" (*A Grief Observed*).

That's not to say we're on our own, by any means. If this were tag-team, all we have to do is "toca la mano." He's there, anxious to help us with spirit, power, and grace, which we access through living faithfully: "For by [you] doing these things, the gates of hell shall not prevail against you; yea, and [when you've invited him,] the Lord God will disperse the powers of darkness from before you and cause the heavens to shake for your good and his name's glory" (D&C 21:6).

The point is this: God's love for you and your love for God ought to motivate you to go out and do good things with your life. It would be a waste of his grace to do anything else. But God leaves it up to us to choose.

Now, lest you think this all rests on you being good enough or always choosing perfectly, let me mention one other point (a point that deserves a book of its own—I can't do it justice here). God is good and gives even to those who have no faith and do nothing to reach toward him. I can attest to it. He has blessed me at the times when I was least deserving.

22. THE IMPORTANCE OF A NAME

Jefferson, you have an awesome name. (In fact, I'd like to name one of my sons after you.) But your name's heritage goes back further than your 16 years.

It started hundreds of years ago as the Germanic *Gottfried*, meaning "God's peace." Its pronunciation shifted when it became *Godfrey*, an Anglo-Saxon tribal surname. *Godfrey* became *Geoffrey* and then *Jeffrey*—till a son of *Jeffrey* became *Jefferson*—which was then a Welsh surname—this was a few centuries ago (I'm not sure it's in our direct ancestry, but we do have Welsh heritage).

The motto attached to the Jefferson crest was the Latin phrase *a cruce salus*, which means "from cross, salvation," or in other words, "salvation comes from the cross"—a pretty cool tribute to the Savior. Perhaps *warcry* is a better word than *motto*. Imagine shouting "A CRUCE SALUS!" as you charge into battle to fight on behalf of *the* King.

This happened to be the surname of one of our American founding fathers too, Thomas Jefferson, a god-fearing man and lover of freedom, the man who said, "The God who gave us life gave us liberty at the same time: The hand of force may destroy, but cannot disjoin them" (this is etched in the marble of the Jefferson Memorial).

These are just three short paragraphs on the name *Jefferson*. But a study of your name and the legacy connected to it could be an entire book—maybe even a series. And yet we can capture all that, at least symbolically, by pronouncing those three short syllables: *JEF·fər·sən*.

Names are important because of what they represent—I once said that to my friend Malori after she told me she didn't know what her name meant. We looked it up together. Turns out it may derive from "unlucky." To rescue her feelings I then had to downplay a name's importance (Shakespeare helps with his "what's in a name?") and remind her of the famous Maloris, like Sir Thomas. It was especially funny because I had a crush on her, which made her name sort of an ill omen. The lesson, though, is to think twice before you pick a name for your kid. Or stop being an English major.

Moving on.

In Acts 13:9, we learn that the apostle Paul had a Latin name as a Roman citizen (which was *Paul*). But he was born an Israelite of the tribe of Benjamin, and his Hebrew name was *Saul* (perhaps named after the ancient king). Why is this important? Well, one of his names identified him as a citizen of one place, and the other identified him as a citizen of another. So his names showed his identity—both where he came from and what he was allowed to do.

Which brings us back to why a name is important—it's tied to the idea of connecting past and future. *Jefferson* has a huge, noble heritage that it represents—the past. But it points to your own future—you have the gift and opportunity to live up to your name. That promise was connected to you from the moment you started breathing.

You have a couple of other names you may not have thought of. You are Jefferson the Mormon. *Mormon* is a nickname we get because a prophet and historian compiled a book about Christ and put his name on it. He got his name from the Waters of Mormon, a place where ancient American Christians promised to take Christ's name upon them. So there's a deep heritage attached to that one simple word—a name.

And that leads to another name you have: Jefferson the Christian—you've taken Christ's name on yourself too. And to be a Christian means more than the general religious association—something vague about how you believe in *The New Testament*. To be a Christian means you "are willing to take upon [you] the name of [God's] son." So you are saying, "Yes, I'm a disciple of the prophet from Nazareth—I'm an acolyte of the Jew who taught us to love our enemies—I'm a soldier for the man who said he was God's firstborn. I follow that man—and I'm so committed to his way of life that I'm calling myself by his name." It means you represent him all the time, even when you're just hanging out in the living room. That name becomes a call for you to live up to. And it also bespeaks your future—as one of Christ's heirs.

23. NAMES THAT CHANGE

When you were born, you were named Jefferson Taylor. The *Taylor* was to match the "JT" of your older brothers. But just before your first birthday, Mom changed your name to Jefferson *Pearce*—after her father, our grandpa. It was a bummer to lose the JT sequence, but your new name is pretty cool—and so is the cowboy heritage it represents. You might research that one too—an Anglo-Saxon name coming from the French *Piers,* which is from the Greek *Petros*, which was the name of Peter, the rock of Christ. The Bible has several examples of special names—names that were so important they were changed too, just like yours.

"Neither shall thy name any more be called Abram, but thy name shall be Abraham; for a father of many nations have I made thee" (Genesis 17:5). God gave this new name to Abraham, and it means "the father of a multitude." So his new name was connected to the new blessings he was then promised. His name and his future were tied together. And the moment they changed—when that Abrahamic promise was made—his future changed with it.

Jacob, his grandson, wrestled with a divine being who asked him, "What is thy name?" When he told him it was Jacob, the being answered, "Thy name shall be called no more Jacob, but Israel: for as a prince hast thou power with God and with men, and hast prevailed." This seems to

suggest that his new name, Israel, meant "prince of God" and was a title that reflected more than his mortal status but something that would last a lot longer (Genesis 32:24-32). Interestingly, Jacob then renamed the place *Peniel,* which means "the face of God." He named it that because "I have seen God face to face, and my life is preserved." If you put the pieces together, it seems God himself appeared to Jacob and gave him a new name—*Israel.* (It also seems he was surprised that he could stand in such overpowering brightness and glory and not be killed by it.)

Isaiah poetically alluded to all Israelites being given a new name (perhaps he was referring to the saints taking Christ's name): "And the Gentiles shall see thy righteousness, and all kings thy glory: and thou shalt be called by a new name, which the mouth of the Lord shall name" (Isaiah 62:2). But what he's saying is that, like he did with Abraham and Jacob, God himself would be renaming his saints.

The Doctrine and Covenants teaches us about an interesting thing that happens in the hereafter: "A white stone is given to each of those who come into the celestial kingdom, whereon is a new name written, which no man knoweth save he that receiveth it. The new name is the key word" (D&C 130:11). But this wasn't a new revelation; rather, it was a clarification of what John had already written nearly two-thousand years before: "He that hath an ear, let him hear... To him that overcometh will I give to eat of the hidden manna, and will give him a white stone, and in the stone a new name written, which no man knoweth saving he that receiveth it" (Revelation 2:17). So at some time, a person will be given a name, from God, that only the person and God will know—a sacred and secret name.

I'm telling you all this about names for one specific reason—you may not have noticed, but this was hidden in the Victor Ludlow quote a few sections back: The point of the initiatory is that you "begin to assume a new spiritual identity, [which is] symbolized with a new name." So part of the initiatory is the receiving of a new name. It's sort of a mortal practice run that seems to represent the divine ceremony that John the Revelator told us to expect in the afterlife.

24. Personal Study

There were some heavy concepts in this chapter. It's a big responsibility to take on, but it's accompanied by beautiful promises. As you prepare for the temple, don't forget that you're preparing to receive both these obligations and the future that goes with them—and that's a good thing.

Scripture

- D&C 76 (The prophet Joseph wrote, "It appeared self-evident from what truths were left [in the Bible], that, if God rewarded every one according to the deeds done in the body, the term *Heaven*, as intended for the Saints' eternal home, must include more kingdoms than one. Accordingly… while translating St. John's Gospel, [we] saw the following vision.")

Sermon

- "Temple Worship" by Elder John A. Widstoe

Go to jwashburn.com/books/dearjeff for links to these readings and a complete bibliography.

Endowment

Teach me, O Lord, the way of thy statutes; and I shall keep it unto the end. Give me understanding, and I shall keep thy law; yea, I shall observe it with my whole heart.

— *Psalms 119:33-34*

25. Endowed

If you keep a sharp eye during a temple open house, you'll notice the endowment takes place in a room full of fixed chairs, which face an altar at the front. So while the initiatory is a very personal ordinance, the endowment is presented to whole groups at a time.

Before you make the covenants of the ordinance (which we'll get to), they teach you about the creation, the fall, and the atonement—which you may have heard called the pillars of the plan of salvation. And you learn these things by following Adam and Eve through the process. Elder Packer described it as

> instruction... [on] dispensations, and the importance of the present as the greatest and grandest era in human history... [It] includes a recital of... the <u>creative period</u>, the condition of our first parents in the <u>Garden of Eden</u>, their disobedience and consequent <u>expulsion</u> from that blissful abode, their condition in the lone and dreary world when doomed to live by labor and sweat, the plan of <u>redemption</u> by which the great transgression may be atoned, the period of the great apostasy, the <u>restoration</u> of the Gospel with all its ancient powers and privileges, the absolute and indispensable condition of personal purity and devotion to the right in present life, and a strict compliance with Gospel requirements. (*The Holy Temple*)

The word *endow* basically means "to gift." An *endowment* is an inherited gift. So in the endowment ceremony a person receives the gift of an inheritance from God. But what does that mean exactly?

I'm sure you remember the concept of *apotheosis* from *The Lost Symbol*—it means to change a man into a god (*apo* = to change; *theos* = god). John explained that this was within Christ's abilities: "As many as received him, to them gave he power to become the sons of God... which were born, not of blood, nor of the will of the flesh, nor of the will of man, but of God" (John 1:12-13).

Moroni spoke of this process before burying his people's record in the ground—his final plea to whoever would be reading it:

> Come unto Christ, and be perfected in him... and if ye shall <u>deny yourselves of all ungodliness</u>, and love God with all your might, mind and strength, then is his grace sufficient for you, that <u>by his grace ye may be perfect</u> in Christ... Then are ye sanctified... through the shedding of the blood of Christ, which is in the covenant of the Father unto the remission of your sins, that <u>ye become holy, without spot</u>. (Moroni 10:32-33)

To become as God is blasphemy if it means to usurp his power and force our way into heaven. And it's blasphemy if it means to become an equal with God too. That would be like a child saying, "Dad, when I grow up you're going to have to scoot over because I'm taking charge of this family." That just isn't the case. A child, even when he has fully grown, will still have a father and still ought to submit to that fatherly wisdom and higher insight.

But God has invited us to become his heirs, to inherit all that he has—not to take his place or overthrow him, but to continue serving under him, as his perfected children. He invites us to partake in the greatest gift he has: to become "heirs of God, and joint-heirs with Christ" (Romans 8:17).

The endowment reminds us that we're God's children and that we're only down here on this rock temporarily. It reminds us that some of the little things don't matter, and some of the things we think are big don't matter either. What does matter, though, is whether we're listening to God's guiding Spirit as it teaches us from the inside how we ought to act.

The endowment teaches us these things, and then it invites us to make covenants that prepare us to receive God's greatest gifts—this apotheosis of his heirs.

TEMPORAL MATTERS: LINGO

When talking about the temple, some people say, "When are you going to *take out* your endowments?" It's not a very good way to phrase it though.

A better way to say it is, "When are you going to *receive* your *endowment?*" (and *endowment* is singular).

---

26. WANDERERS, STRANGERS, AND PILGRIMS

I mentioned earlier that you might imagine yourself as a Christian soldier. Taking on that identity can help you see your noble purpose, which is often obscured and scorned by the world. When you think of that soldier archetype, you probably think of verbs like *striving* and *fighting*. The soldier disciple is a warrior, one who endures, who marches, who stands forth and holds fast.

I'd like to suggest another archetype, one whose cloak you might also put on. This character is the *wanderer*.

Imagine a noble vagabond, a hero dressed in rags—not because he doesn't take care of himself, but because he's gone through so much for so many miles. When you think of the wanderer archetype, you might think of verbs like *dream* and *hope*. The wanderer is a disciple who has vision and insight—a pilgrim who both imagines and seeks illumination, which he knows will simply be the home he longs for—one greater than he can comprehend.

And so that we don't fragment our storyline too far, let me quickly mention a term you probably already know, one that reminds me of the round table: The term is *knight errant*. *Errant* is an adjective meaning "wandering or roving." So it's possible to be a soldier of Christ and a vagabond at the same time. These errant knights would strike out into the open world without a specific aim other than to somehow prove their chivalry by doing good when they came upon a situation where they could help. They may have already had heroic hearts back at court, but they needed to prove those hearts through heroic *deeds*. To find these proving situations, they had to wander. And they didn't return home till their wandering quests were somehow fulfilled.

The scriptures support this archetype in a slightly different way, the most classic example being the children of Israel. Israel, the grandson of Abraham (whose name, as we discussed, was changed from Jacob), thought his son Joseph was dead. Then one day in his old age, his sons returned from Egypt with the news that Joseph was alive. Israel traveled with his whole family (around 70 people) to Egypt, where they were honored as guests. When Israel died not long after, Joseph took his father's body and buried it back in their homeland. But then Joseph returned to Egypt where he lived till he died. In fact, Israel's descendants stayed for a couple hundred years, till their numbers were large. The new pharaoh, wanting to keep them in check, turned them into slaves and made life pretty miserable for them. Their prayers invited God to raise up a deliverer, Moses, to lead them out of there.

So why is this important?

Their deliverance was only necessary because they had lived in Egypt long enough to get comfortable there—even though it wasn't their real home. In fact, because their stay in Egypt was supposed to be short, the Lord had called it a "sojourn" (Isaiah 52:4), which, by definition, is a short stay. But the Israelites didn't sojourn. They dug in their roots, or hammered in their stakes, in a way that made it hard for them to leave. You might say that they forgot where they were really from.

It's a metaphor of our own spiritual journey: We left the presence of our Father in heaven to come to earth so we could navigate the proving ground. But we often get so comfortable down here that we forget what we're doing—and that we won't be here for long. In fact, we've all become so completely stuck that it's impossible for us to escape on our own. We need a deliverer, a Moses—someone who can lead us out, who can redeem us with powers beyond our own.

These stories of wanderers play the important role of reminding us that we're sojourners, here for a bit, but not for long. This metaphor is spread throughout the scriptures under different names: *wanderers*, *strangers*, and *pilgrims*:

- **Deuteronomy 10:19** "<u>Love ye therefore the stranger: for ye were strangers</u> in the land of Egypt."
- **Psalms 119:19** "<u>I am a stranger in the earth</u>: hide not thy commandments from me."
- **Luke 15:11-14** "A certain man had two sons: And the younger of them said to his father, Father, give me the portion of goods that falleth to me. And he divided unto them his living. And not many days after the younger son gathered all together, and <u>took his journey into a far country</u>, and there wasted his substance with riotous living. And when he had spent all, there arose a mighty famine in that land; and he began to be in want."
- **Hebrews 11:8-10** "By faith Abraham, when he was called to go out into a place which he should after receive for an inheritance, obeyed; and he went out, not knowing whither he went. By faith <u>he sojourned in the land of promise, as in a strange country, dwelling in tabernacles</u> with Isaac and Jacob, the heirs with him of the same promise: For <u>he looked for a city</u> which hath foundations, <u>whose builder and maker is God</u>."
- **Hebrews 11:13** "These all died in faith, not having received the promises, but having seen them afar off, and were persuaded of them, and embraced them, and <u>confessed that they were strangers and pilgrims</u> on the earth."
- **1 Peter 2:11** "<u>I beseech you as strangers and pilgrims</u>, abstain from fleshly lusts, which war against the soul."

- **Jacob 7:26** "And it came to pass that I, Jacob, began to be old; and the record of this people being kept on the other plates of Nephi, wherefore, I conclude this record, declaring that I have written according to the best of my knowledge, by saying that the time passed away with us, and also <u>our lives passed away like as it were unto us a dream</u>, we being a <u>lonesome</u> and a solemn people, <u>wanderers</u>, cast out from Jerusalem, born in tribulation, <u>in a wilderness</u>, and hated of our brethren, which caused wars and contentions; wherefore, we did mourn out our days." (There are a lot of beautiful farewells from the writers of *The Book of Mormon*, but I think that's my favorite.)
- **Alma 13:23** "[The glad tidings] are made known unto us in plain terms, that we may understand, that we cannot err; and this <u>because of our being wanderers in a strange land</u>; therefore, we are thus highly favored, for we have these glad tidings declared unto us in all parts of our vineyard."
- **Alma 26:36** "Now if this is boasting, even so will I boast; for this is my life and my light, my joy and my salvation, and my redemption from everlasting woe. Yea, blessed is the name of my God, who has been mindful of this people, who are a branch of the tree of <u>Israel</u>, and <u>has been lost from its body</u>... yea, I say, blessed be the name of my God, who has been mindful of us, <u>wanderers in a strange land</u>.
- **D&C 45:13** "And [the people of Enoch] <u>confessed they were strangers and pilgrims</u> on the earth." (Interesting that it was something they *confessed*—as if not everyone has the mettle to admit it.)

- **D&C 25:10** "<u>Lay aside the things of this world</u>, and <u>seek for the things of a better</u>."

I think that last one is my favorite.

There is a better world—really—than this one we see all around us. And instead of looking for that better world, we sometimes get caught up in the one we can see—unable to lay it aside. But if we can remember that we're just wanderers here, we'll keep our focus on "the things of a better."

A good Muslim, according to the five pillars of Islam, is supposed to make at least one pilgrimage to Mecca in his lifetime—a journey called the *hajj*. Christians have been making pilgrimages to the Holy Land for centuries, eager to walk in the footsteps of Christ, literally following his path. And Christ himself was a wanderer, who came down unto his own from heaven, but his own received him not. The British poet James Montgomery named Christ "a poor, wayfaring man of grief" (a wayfarer is one who travels, especially on foot). Your experience in the temple will be the same sort of journey—taking up the pilgrim's mantle, the rags of a wanderer.

Daniel C. Petersen is one of BYU's top religious scholars and a personable gentleman too (I recommend his lecture "Understanding Islam"). These are his thoughts on the theme of wanderers:

> Most pilgrimage is associated with special rituals and ceremonies. Pilgrims are often required to don sacred robes and undergo spiritual exercises such as prayer, reading scriptures, or meditation. Many pilgrims abstain from ordinary activities of life by fasting, sleepless vigils, or sexual abstinence. Sacrifice

or offerings are often required of the pilgrim, even if it is only placing a flower or rock in a special place. In return many pilgrims obtain tokens of their pilgrimages—special clothing, jewelry, books, medallions, or relics—which they proudly wear or display as symbolic of their spiritual status as pilgrims.

The endowment ceremony is this sort of pilgrimage. It's a small journey that represents our larger quest to return to the place we belong—man's odyssey from premortality to eternity. In the endowment, we symbolically ascend, looking toward that day when we will actually ascend. And that journey becomes a reminder and a guide.

As Abraham wrote, "Eternity was our covering and our rock and our salvation, as we *journeyed*" (Abraham 2:16).

27. BLESSINGS OF THE FALL

You blink your eyes and squint.

You push your hands into the mud and raise your face out of a brown puddle. A wagon wheel rolls past on your right side, nearly crushing your hand. An old man wearing a sou'wester rain hat, laughs loudly, exposing his rotting teeth. You lean back till you're kneeling, and look up at the raindrops spiking down.

And you realize you don't even know your own name.

An old woman tells you, unbelievable as it is, that she saw you falling down with the torrents of rain. You hesitate to believe her, and yet you have no other explanation.

This is how the wanderer's story begins—he can't remember his past, and his future looks a little murky. If you read his whole story, he eventually comes to realize that he *does* have a past—a noble one, in fact. He only learns of this, though, by piecing together the fragments he discovers as he travels.

You and I are the same way—we wake up one day and realize we don't recognize this mortal terrain all around us. Or maybe it's that we know, somehow, that there's more to it than this—that we must have come *from somewhere*. Luckily, we've found scrolls that reveal some shards of what came before—one in particular from Abraham's journal, talking about who we were before we were born:

> God saw these souls... were good, and he stood in the midst of them, and he said: "These I will make my rulers;" for he stood among those that were spirits... and he said unto me: "Abraham, thou art one of them; thou wast chosen before thou wast born."
> And there stood one among them that was like unto God, and he said unto those who were with him: "We will go down, for there is space there, and we will take of these materials, and we will make an earth whereon these may dwell; And we will prove them herewith, to see if they will do all things whatsoever the Lord their God shall command them." (Abraham 3:23-25)

These few short verses give us important clues about where we're from and why we're here. The endowment does too—it teaches us about the part of our lives that we can't remember. This is valuable because it reminds us of the long view—the eternal perspective.

As we learn about our past, we learn about the creation—how it all began. Creation is fairly straightforward (because we're not discussing whether Adam had a belly button or whether God set up the most impressive domino chain ever—one that took 13.7 billion years—even if it is interesting speculation). Basically, we owe the existence of all life to God, who instructed Christ and others to organize the universe and everything in it. (As another side note, do you know Christ's three most important roles? He *was* the creator, he *is* the redeemer, and he *will be* the judge.)

The family proclamation teaches us that "Sacred ordinances and covenants available in holy temples make it possible for individuals to return to the presence of God." Notice it says *return*—echoing the idea that we used to be in God's presence before we landed in the mud. That was the state of Adam after the creation: God had sent him through a veil that left him with no memory of his former existence, starting him on earth with a blank slate—a *tabula rasa*. His object in this life was to cross back through that veil. While we're here in mortal probation, that long view—including our former knowledge—is just out of our reach, "for now we see through a glass, darkly." But when we return to meet our Father, it will be "face to face: now I know in part; but then shall I know even as also I am known" (1 Corinthians 13:12).

Sometime after the creation, Adam and Eve made the choice that resulted in the fall—which is not quite so clear-cut as the creation. A lot of people, including C. S. Lewis, saw the fall as a negative thing—something it would have been nice to avoid. (One of my favorite of Lewis's books is a sci-fi novel called *Out of the Silent Planet*; its sequel, *Perelandra*, is about an earth-like world on the verge of falling—all based on a doctrinal misunderstanding.) Even

with modern revelation, it's easy to come to some wrong conclusions, so let's review some of the fundamentals.

We've discussed the importance of symbolism, especially in the temple ceremony. The story of the fall may be much more symbolic than literal—even the fruit might be a metaphor. That's an important thing to keep in mind as you're pondering. Having said that though,

> The Fall [itself]... <u>was a historical event that literally occurred</u> in the history of man. Many points in latter-day revelation are also clarified that are not discernible from the Bible... [particularly] that <u>the Fall is a blessing and that Adam and Eve should be honored</u> in their station as the first parents of the earth. (Bible Dictionary: The Fall)

In other words, the fall really happened (we just don't know how it happened exactly), and it was a good thing. You may have noticed that quote was from the Bible Dictionary, which is always a great place to start (remember that when you're a missionary). It goes on to explain:

> The Fall of Adam and Eve <u>is one of the most important occurrences in the history of man</u>. Before the Fall, there were no sin, no death, and no children... After Adam fell, the whole creation fell and became mortal [too]. Adam's Fall brought both physical and spiritual death into the world upon all mankind.

From that, we get the idea that the fall initiated three things: sin, death, and the ability to have children. The first two seem like bad things, but the third is obviously good. Because it brought sin and death, the fall ignited the great battle between good and evil on this mortal world. Before that, there wasn't a conflict. Afterwards, as we've discussed with the soldier metaphor, a real battle raged, with two great forces pitted against each other:

> And [Enoch] beheld Satan... [who] had a great chain in his hand, and it veiled the whole face of the earth with darkness; and [Satan] looked up and laughed, and his angels rejoiced. And Enoch beheld angels descending out of heaven, bearing testimony of the Father and Son; and the Holy Ghost fell on many, and they were caught up by the powers of heaven into Zion. (Moses 7:26-27)

That visual of Satan and his angels looking up and laughing is powerful and frightening. It sounds like an epic tale: The Prince of Darkness leads demons up from below to grasp the ankles of the mortals, while the Father of Light, mighty scepter in hand, sends his angels from heaven to help the mortals rise. The fall caused that battle—it took God's children out of the safe zone, where they could neither rise nor sink, and set them in no-man's land with bullets whizzing by their ears. Why would God have done this—allowing sin to come into the world?

You and I just watched March Madness together. More than 64 teams went into the tournament, and Louisville came out on top. That was a huge victory for them—to rise over so many great teams. Imagine if Louisville had played against 64 high school teams. It wouldn't have meant anything if they'd won *that*—it would have been an empty victory. But that wasn't the case. Their victory was great because their opponents were great.

It's the same for us in this life—God allows the bad guys onto the court so we have a worthy opponent to prove ourselves against. It's not that he's rooting for them—he's definitely not. He just wants to give us the chance for a real victory. As Lehi taught Jacob in his farewell speech, there needs to be "an opposition in all things," because without it, you can't have righteousness, or holiness, or good of any kind—no true victories (2 Nephi 2:11). Without it, creation would be indifferent and neutral, never filling any sort of purpose, "a thing of naught," which is why "it must needs be that there was an opposition" (2 Nephi 2:15). The Lord set up the creation so it would result in the fall—he planned it that way:

> The Fall was no surprise to the Lord. It was a necessary step in the progress of man, and provisions for a Savior had been made even before the Fall had occurred. Jesus Christ came to atone for the Fall of Adam and also for man's individual sins. (Bible Dictionary: The Fall)

It wouldn't make sense if God were surprised when the fall happened. And since he knew it was coming, he would have stopped it if he'd thought it was a bad thing. But he didn't—he allowed it to happen. And he'd already set up a solution—a deliverer, the Savior of the world.

I'm a writer—a wordsmith—which is why I keep telling you about the roots (i.e. *etymology*) of words. It's just sort of a natural drive that I have—not sure why. But it's that drive that one day got me thinking about what exactly the word *transgress* meant. I connected it to a bunch of other, similar words, illustrating them with simple lines,

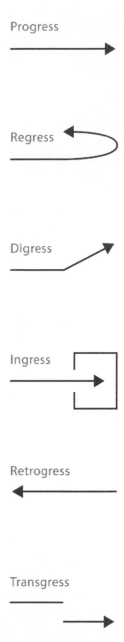

Progress

Regress

Digress

Ingress

Retrogress

Transgress

each having to do with movement (you tell me whether I assigned the arrows accurately).

Transgression was a change (*trans*) in forward motion, but it continued as forward motion. It was just a new type of forward motion, different (and now separate) from what had come before. As Lehi put it: "Adam fell that men might be; and men are, that they might have joy" (2 Nephi 2:27). His transgression was the change we humans needed to keep moving forward.

Encountering sin was a huge risk. But, like a good coach, God made sure Adam and Eve were prepared, and, along with providing a Savior, he sent help:

> I, the Lord God, gave unto Adam and unto his seed, that they should not die as to the temporal death, until I, the Lord God, should send forth angels to declare unto them repentance and redemption, through faith on the name of mine Only Begotten Son. And thus did I, the Lord God, appoint unto man the days of his probation—that by

his natural death he might be raised in immortality unto eternal life, even as many as would believe. (D&C 29:42-43)

In other words, he sent prophets to teach the plan to us, to help us get past the ignorance and innocence created by the veil. God testified directly to prophets, so that they knew as sure as anything. Then he asked them to tell the world—which they have done directly and through writing their testimonies.

After Adam and Eve were kicked out of the garden, they were sent into the crumbling, dangerous, mortal world, which I'm sure was tough. But they were still aware of the good that came from it:

Adam blessed God and was filled [with the Spirit], and began to prophesy concerning all the families of the earth, saying: Blessed be the name of God, for because of my transgression [1] my eyes are opened, and [2] in this life I shall have joy, and again [3] in the flesh I shall see God. And Eve, his wife, heard all these things and was glad, saying: Were it not for our transgression we never should [4] have had seed, and never should [5] have known good and evil, and [6] the joy of our redemption, and the (7) eternal life which God giveth unto all the obedient. (Moses 5:10-11)

So, to wrap up, the creation was Act I. It prepared the conditions for the fall and man's probationary period—an essential part of man's progression. The fall, in turn, was meant to be concluded by the atonement. Any discussion of the fall is ultimately glorifying God's greatest gift to us—his Only Begotten Son.

28. The Path of Righteousness

LDSChurchTemples.com points out something unique to the Salt Lake Temple:

> [It] features beautiful hand-painted murals on the walls of its progressive-style ordinance rooms: Creation Room, Garden Room, World Room, Terrestrial Room (no murals), and Celestial Room (no murals). [It] is one of only seven temples where patrons progress through four ordinance rooms before passing into the Celestial Room.

As you go through the endowment ceremony in the Salt Lake Temple, you progress from room to room. The other six temples that have this architecture are Manti, Laie Hawaii, Cardston, Idaho Falls, Los Angeles, and Nauvoo. All other temples use a more compact format, which trade a little bit of clarity for efficiency. Luckily, and I recommend this, you can go to the Salt Lake temple sometime to get this experience that you don't get elsewhere. (Also, LDS.org's "Inside the Temple" has images of the interior.)

The symbolic progression is an important part of the temple ceremony. If you look real close at the model of the Salt Lake Temple, you'll see that the consecutive rooms spiral upward (starting with the baptismal font at the bottom left). Each is at least a little higher than the previous—even when two are on the same floor. And you

progress upward till you reach the celestial room. (I should also point out that this unique temple has an assembly room for the Apostles and Seventy—the large room above the ordinance rooms.) Hugh Nibley said the ancient Egyptians had this same symbolic upward walk in their temples. You'll notice it too in the ancient Israelite temples—a stairway marks the passage from one segment to another. And all of this mirrors Adam and Eve's journey, rising from the fallen state and returning to the presence of God.

The *Encyclopedia of Mormonism* describes the progression a little more directly:

> For the instructions and ordinances within [the Salt Lake Temple], a processional plan is followed through

several rooms, each signifying a stage in man's path of eternal progression. Each room is decorated with murals depicting that stage of the journey. First is the Creation Room, where the <u>creative periods of the earth</u> are considered. Next, the <u>events of Eden</u> are the subject in the Garden Room. The World (or Telestial) Room depicts <u>conditions following the expulsion</u> of Adam and Eve from the Garden of Eden, providing a background for the Atonement of Christ, the great apostasy, and the restoration of the gospel. In the Terrestrial Room, <u>the requirements of the pure life and of complete commitment</u> to the work of the Lord are taught. The path then leads <u>through the veil</u> of the Temple to the Celestial Room, representing <u>the "heaven of heavens,"</u> the glorious kingdom of God.

[By the way, the *Encyclopedia of Mormonism* is now an online resource hosted by BYU: http://eom.byu.edu/.]

Alma said, "I perceive that ye are in the path which leads to the kingdom of God" (Alma 7:19). We, God's wandering children, are away from home. The endowment is a way to illuminate the path we need to follow. And it includes a literal path that leads us upward.

TEMPORAL MATTERS: LIVE SESSIONS

LDSChurchTemples.com also says that "The Salt Lake Temple is one of two temples that still employs live acting for presentation of the endowment." The other is the Manti temple.

In all other temples, the endowment's format has been changed to a movie, which, as I mentioned before, is for efficiency. The movie is great, but it's interesting and informative to see the endowment presented live. I recommend you plan a trip to Salt Lake or Manti for this reason specifically.

---

29. THE COVENANTS

If you remember, my friend from the introduction said he wished he'd known what promises he was going to make before he was asked to make them—which doesn't seem like an unreasonable request. But people are generally very hesitant to speak about the covenants because they know the temple ceremony is so sacred. Luckily, there are a few reliable sources that cover the covenants—sources I can comfortably cite without feeling like I've said too much.

James E. Talmage, the Apostle who wrote *Jesus the Christ* (which you definitely ought to read, although maybe in a year or two—it's not exactly light reading), mentioned several of the temple covenants. I've numbered them here too—but in the order of their sequence in the actual ceremony:

> The ordinances of the endowment embody certain obligations on the part of the individual, such as the covenant and promise [3] <u>to observe the law of strict virtue and chastity</u>, [2] <u>to be charitable, benevolent, tolerant and pure</u>; [4] <u>to devote both talent and material means to the spread of truth</u> and the uplifting of the race; to maintain devotion to the cause of truth; and to seek in every way to contribute to the great preparation that the earth may be made ready to receive her King—the Lord Jesus Christ. <u>With the taking of each covenant and the assuming of each obligation, a promised blessing is pronounced, contingent upon the faithful observance of the conditions</u>... In every detail the endowment ceremony contributes to covenants of morality of life, consecration of person to high ideals, devotion to truth, patriotism to nation, and allegiance to God. (*The House of the Lord* 100)

Hugh Nibley, in his *A House of Glory*, described them this way:

> When I ask what the temple teaches me, the answer is loud and clear: to control my actions. That is

self-discipline and that is what I promise to exercise with every covenant. The [1] <u>law of sacrifice</u> requires me to do things I could more easily not do; the [2] <u>law of the gospel</u> requires self-control in everyday situations, avoiding the same unseeming acts as are condemned in the instructions of the Dead Sea Scrolls, such as laughing too loudly, gossiping, and immodest dress. That [3] <u>chastity</u> is nothing but self-control needs no argument. And the hardest of all, the [4] <u>law of consecration</u>, can only be faced against sore temptation, and still confronts us with unresolved dilemmas. What I promise to do with every covenant is to order my life.

Now some of these sources can seem old and outdated—especially when they're Apostles and saints who died before you were born. Well, here's one from a year ago, April 2012, just a few days before you turned sixteen—Elder Robert D. Hales said this in front of the whole world:

As endowed temple recommend holders, we establish patterns of Christlike living. These include [0] <u>obedience</u>, [1] making <u>sacrifices</u> to keep the commandments, [2] <u>loving</u> one another, [3] being <u>chaste</u> in thought and action, and [4] <u>giving of ourselves to build the kingdom of God</u>. Through the Savior's Atonement and by following these basic patterns of faithfulness, we receive "power from on high" to face the challenges of life. We need this divine power today more than ever. It is power we receive only through temple ordinances. I testify that the sacrifices we make to receive temple ordinances are worth every effort we can make.

The truth is, I think many endowed members didn't even notice he laid it out so clearly. But he did. In other words, the temple covenants are available to those who look, but they're usually not spotlighted directly. Match the numbers in this quote with the previous quotes, and you'll have an even clearer picture.

And that picture invites us to zoom in on the pieces for a closer look.

30. Obedience

When Moses exited the biblical stage, Joshua was called to take his place as leader. After Joshua reminded the Israelites that they needed to complete the job Moses started, which was inheriting the promised land, they responded with,

> All that thou commandest us we will do, and whithersoever thou sendest us, we will go. According as we hearkened unto Moses in all things, so will we hearken unto thee: only the Lord thy God be with thee, as he was with Moses. (Joshua 1:16-17)

Basically, they said they'd do whatever he asked them to—they were confirming to him that they supported him as their leader. In the church sometimes they call this *sustaining* someone, and the Israelites sustained Joshua. Except they did it with one caveat—the last phrase of that quote: "We'll follow you just as long as the Lord God is with you, like he always was with Moses." They were willing to do anything he asked—basically unconditional obedience, except for that one condition—that he stay aligned with God's will.

If we're going to put faith in a Joshua, we need to have faith in the God that he's following—we have to trust God first. We trust him because of three of his basic attributes: He wants us to be happy in the long run, he knows everything, and he has power to do anything. Because God is like this, we can put full confidence in him. And as long as Joshua is following God, we can put full confidence in him too (even when it seems to contradict our own desires)—just like the Israelites did.

The Israelites said they would *hearken* to Joshua, which is a word some people get hung up on in a big way. Honestly, I doubt it'll be a problem for you, but you may be able to reach out to others who struggle with it, so I'll keep explaining. (By the way, a majority of the revelations in *The Doctrine and Covenants* start with "hearken.")

You can see the word *hear* embedded in *hearken*. It simply means to have your ears open—something all Christians should do. As Jacob puts it, "Wo unto the deaf that will not hear; for they shall perish" (2 Nephi 9:31). It's simply a matter of being open-minded instead of closed-minded. But the issue isn't necessarily simple: We Christians are supposed to have the truth and stick to it—holding on to what's right even when society throws morals out the window. But that can lead to our being closed-minded and prideful, which is wrong—a pretty big type of wrong too. Along with holding fast to the truth, we're supposed to be humble enough to admit when we're wrong about *what we thought the truth was.* It's a careful line to walk, but the key is to stop thinking of yourself as such a big deal.

Now, let's link *hearken* to the word *commandment*, which I sometimes take issue with. *Command* is a word they use in computer lingo. When you give a computer a command, it has to obey (though we're talking about basic code rather than getting Windows to do what you want—which is a whole nother beast, ha ha). A computer doesn't have a choice whether to do the command or not—it doesn't have free will: it's simply programmed to follow instructions. And sometimes people think the Lord's commandments are the same sort of thing—like we simply have to obey these arbitrary rules—in other words, "Do what *I* command or *I'm* going to punish you," and we're supposed to obey like mindless computers. Looking at it this way, commandments are a very selfish thing for God to do. But we're humans—children of God—not mindless programs. And, fortunately, God's commandments are quite a bit different than what you'd give to a program:

First, a commandment isn't mandatory like it is with a computer. God could force your hand if he wanted to, but he doesn't. He lets us choose—every time. "Thou shalt not kill" was in effect when Cain murdered Abel, but God thought allowing free will was more important than saving Abel's life (which goes to show how important freedom is by God's reckoning).

Second, God doesn't reserve punishment for punishment's sake: "You did such and such? Well that's 39 lashings then." That's not it at all. Instead, commandments are simply the guidelines for being happy. As Nephi put it again, "We lived after the manner of happiness" (2 Nephi

5:27). Nephi was saying, "There's a way to live happy, and we simply followed the pattern." Hearkening to God doesn't mean we're becoming mindless lemmings who just follow blindly. Instead it means we're smart enough and independent enough that we're willing to listen to good advice—especially when that advice is teaching us how to be happy. So we're using our God-given freedom to choose the pattern of happiness.

Now that we've got a pretty good foundation for obeying God, let's look more in depth at obeying Joshua. Or in our case it could be a prophet who recommends no more than just one earring per ear; or maybe it's someone more lowly still, like your bishop, who's just a regular guy (even though he's a representative of Christ on the earth—a shepherd of part of Christ's flock).

I want you to visualize this: Imagine what God wants—his *will*—is represented by a black line running horizontally across the whiteboard. If the bishop is hearkening to God, then what the bishop wants will be a line that runs perfectly over the top of the first. And that means hearkening to the bishop is the exact same as hearkening to God. There could be a case, though, when the bishop's will isn't aligned with God's—in that case the two lines will only intersect at one small point. If this is ever the case, it's best to put the bishop's words aside and still follow God's will. That is to say, we're responsible to follow our leaders only so far as they follow God—just like the Israelites and Joshua.

Having said that, it's important to remember that we humans are fallible (please don't forget humility—bringing yourself low). When you think of your bishop, you might think, "It's clear that no bishop is perfect, so I better be careful about how and when I follow." But we ought not to point that criticism at others until we've used it all up on ourselves. We are probably not so keen as we think, and we're more likely to be mistaken in that assumption than correct. So if there's even a shred of doubt as to whether you're *right* in assuming the leader is *wrong*, it's probably best to follow your priesthood leader anyway. We have to be careful not to let pride tell us that we're right and someone else is wrong. Pride is the great sin, after all.

Let's shift gears just a little now. Instead of the bishop-and-saint relationship, let's talk about husband and wife. The letter to the Ephesians says something along these lines, and it makes some people's blood boil (not yours or mine though):

> Wives, submit yourselves unto your own husbands, as unto the Lord. For the husband is the head of the wife, even as Christ is the head of the church: and he is the saviour of the body. Therefore as the church is subject unto Christ, so let the wives be to their own husbands in every thing. Husbands, love your wives, even as Christ also loved the church, and gave himself for it. (Ephesians 5:22-25)

Women might rightly get upset at this, *if*—and this is a big *if*—if it means that women have to follow commands like computer programs. But this isn't what it means. It just means women should have their ears open when their husbands have the black lines of their wills on the same path as God's. Hopefully this is a comfort to women. It ought to be.

Now, to the men. If there's any man that thinks he has

the right to boss anyone around, he's got another thing coming. Joseph Smith wrote this in a letter from Liberty Jail:

> We have learned by sad experience that it is the nature and disposition of almost all men, as soon as they get a little authority, as they suppose, they will immediately begin to exercise unrighteous dominion. (D&C 121:39)

He's right: it *is* sad.

Coincidentally, the same natural tendencies that nudge a man toward unrighteous dominion will also make him think, "It says *'almost all men,'* and I'm not one of those who have that disposition." I'm guilty of thinking this myself (but I'm trying not to). Either way, it's a safe bet to assume that if you think Joseph *wasn't* talking about you, you're a ripe candidate. Better to be sorrowful and humbly ask, "Lord, is it I?" (Matthew 26:21-25).

C. S. Lewis commented on that Ephesian scripture too, and he turns it around, just as Christ would have done, so that he who would be great is made into the least and the servant of all:

> Christian writers have sometimes spoken of the husband's headship with a complacency to make the blood run cold. We must go back to our Bibles. The husband is the head of the wife just in so far as he is to her what Christ is to the Church. He is to love her as Christ loved the Church—read on—and *give his life* for her. This headship, then, is most fully embodied not in the husband we should all wish to be, but in

him whose marriage is most like a crucifixion... (*The Four Loves* 105)

That's a powerful thought. But it rings true. We should strive to be husbands willing to be crucified even, in the service of our wives. At the least, we ought to be willing to forget about what we want—"Not my will, but thine be done" (Luke 22:42)—like Christ.

We should strive for this sort of submissiveness in marriage and as we approach God himself. James the brother of the Lord advised: "Humble yourselves in the sight of the Lord, and he shall lift you up" (James 4:10). In other words, like the Christian paradox, we need to lose ourselves in order to find our true selves. And submitting our own wants in a marriage will help us to learn to submit more perfectly to deity, which isn't nearly as easy as it sounds:

> Christ says, "Give me All. I don't want so much of your time and so much of your money and so much of your work: I want *You*. I have not come to torment your natural self, but to kill it. No half-measures are any good. I don't want to cut off a branch here and a branch there; I want to have the whole tree down... hand over the whole natural self, all the desires which you think innocent as well as the ones you think wicked—the whole outfit. I will give you a new self instead. In fact, I will give you *Myself*: my own will shall become yours." (C. S. Lewis, *Mere Christianity* 167)

Like I said, it's a tough thing to do—to lose ourselves.

But that's what we're shooting for. King Benjamin's people promised to do it:

> We are willing to enter into a covenant with our God to *do his will,* and to be obedient to his commandments in all things that he shall command us, all the remainder of our days. (Mosiah 5:5)

And the Lord has promised he'll bless and give gifts to anyone who does:

> But inasmuch as there are those who have hearkened unto my words, I have prepared a blessing and an endowment for them, if they continue faithful. (D&C 105:18)

31. SACRIFICE

Obedience is a logical first step. We need to be willing to obey—to follow God's recommendations—before it does us any good for him to give us the rest. But, before we dive into these others, I want to mention a couple other purposes that commandments serve, along with teaching us the happiest way to live. The Lord explained to the Israelites why he commanded them to go through the wilderness:

> Thou shalt remember all the way which the Lord thy God led thee these forty years in the wilderness, to humble thee, and to prove thee, to know what was in thine heart, whether thou wouldest keep his commandments, or no. (Deuteronomy 8:2)

First, notice the word *remember*—which is key, and we'll

talk more about that in a bit. Next he says the purpose was *to humble*, which we just talked about—allowing ourselves to be brought low. It was also *to prove*—to see what their hearts were made of—just like the knights errant. That leads well into the first commandment we're asked to obey in the temple: sacrifice.

Right after Adam and Eve got kicked out of the garden, they were asked to sacrifice the firstborn of their flocks—it was a thing they did often, for a long time. So while they got settled in and had some kids, they continually obeyed that commandment:

> And after many days an angel of the Lord appeared unto Adam, saying: Why dost thou offer sacrifices unto the Lord? And Adam said unto him: I know not, save the Lord commanded me. (Moses 5:6)

Just real quick, I want to point out something: Adam said, "There's one thing I don't know, and that's why exactly the Lord asked me to do this. But there's something else that I *do* know, and that's that the Lord, who's perfect, asked me to do it." His faith, I'd argue, was based on that second thing—the thing he knew—rather than the thing he didn't know. So it wasn't blind faith at all. Faith is based on knowledge. But this is off topic. We were talking about how an angel appeared to Adam. And since there was something Adam didn't know, the angel cleared it up for him:

> This thing is a similitude of the sacrifice of the Only Begotten of the Father, which is full of grace and truth. Wherefore, thou shalt do all that thou doest in the name of the Son, and thou shalt repent and

call upon God in the name of the Son forevermore. (Moses 5:7-8)

So basically its purpose was to remind Adam of Christ—again, remembering is important. And because Adam obeyed the law of sacrifice, he got the natural consequence:

> And in that day the Holy Ghost fell upon Adam, which beareth record of the Father and the Son, saying: I am the Only Begotten of the Father from the beginning, henceforth and forever, that as thou hast fallen thou mayest be redeemed, and all mankind, even as many as will. (Moses 5:9)

Adam lived the guidelines of happiness, and that naturally yielded certain fruits. In this case, he was living the guideline called sacrifice, and it brought him a stronger testimony of the Savior's ability to heal him.

As we sacrifice, we give up what we want, which helps us to get over ourselves. Giving up what we want changes us—it molds us into better people. That's why it's so hard to do. But this shaping is precisely what this life is for.

> A religion that does not require the sacrifice of all things never has power sufficient to produce the faith necessary unto life and salvation. (Joseph Smith, *Lectures on Faith*)

And it's important to note that the law of sacrifice has embedded in it the promise of a Savior who would be the great and last sacrifice. As we give up things for the Lord, we should remember that God gave up his own son for our benefit.

32. Holiness

Remember the Tibetan monks we walked with at the beginning? There's something admirable about their manner—the way they conduct themselves as they interact (or don't interact) with the world at large. Their leader is known as His Holiness the Dalai Lama. The name is a little mysterious to us westerners, maybe in a way that will surprise you. *Dalai Lama* means "the ocean of wisdom." Once you know the translation, it's a fairly straightforward concept—the truth he knows is both wide and deep, expansive enough to overwhelm you. But that's not all of it. We westerners tacked on "His Holiness" to the beginning of his title, so there's no way to simplify it by interpretation—it began and ended in our language. And, to me, that's harder to pin down than the other part. What exactly does it mean to be holy?

Christ asked the members of his church to manifest, "by a godly walk and conversation, that they are worthy [of being called Christians], that there may be works and faith agreeable to the holy scriptures—walking in holiness before the Lord" (D&C 20:69). He called this thing "a godly walk." In other words, if you're going to be known by Christ's name, you better act like he did—you've got to do more than just talk big. We might say, then, that *holiness* means behaving in a divine manner, or doing what Christ would do. (When I was a kid, the popular evangelical WWJD bracelets reminded people, "What would Jesus do?")

The verb *sanctify* comes from the Latin noun *sanctus*, and it means "to make holy." The Lord promised his servants: "Ye are to be taught from on high. [So] sanctify yourselves and ye shall be endowed with power" (D&C 43:16). If you think about it, he's saying you'll have a god as your teacher—I'm not sure how to emphasize the magnitude of that. It's huge. And to be worthy of that, he says to make yourself holy.

So how can we act like Christ without hanging out with him once in awhile to learn what he's like? Well, the scriptures teach us about his holy attributes. Much of it is about avoiding things that are *unholy*. We're supposed to "Keep [our] tongue from evil, and [our] lips from speaking guile" (Psalms 34:13). We're supposed to lay aside "all malice, and all guile, and hypocrisies, and envies, and all evil speakings" (1 Peter 2:1). We're supposed to "cast away [our] idle thoughts and [our] excess of laughter" (D&C 88:69).

That's an interesting one, and I'd like to linger on it for a moment. *The Doctrine and Covenants* says to live in "thanksgiving, with cheerful hearts... not with much laughter, for this is sin, but with a glad heart and a cheerful countenance" (D&C 59:15). So laughing too much, or being too light minded, can be a problem—it distracts us from truer happiness.

When I was about six, I remember our cousin Jazzie asking me, "Are you okay? You seem gloomy." I was shocked that she'd noticed, and I tried right away to fake like I was happy. But I wasn't, and it wasn't for any particular reason either. I didn't know why I felt sad—I just did. Even when I was that young I had a melancholy personality. (And I took heart a little when Mormon called himself "a sober child." *I* was certainly a sober child.) It's something that I've struggled to overcome through the years. To counter the gloom, I've tried to be more jovial. Our brother Tanner,

I think, is the perfect counterpoint: He always seems to have something funny to say.

I've sought for laughter as an antidote. Tanner seems gifted with it. And yet these scriptures are warning us about it. I guess, like many things, it's a little bit complicated in practice. I, for one, probably need more laughter in my life—to stop taking everything so seriously. Elder Richard G. Scott said this in April 2012's conference:

> A good sense of humor helps revelation; loud laughter does not: A sense of humor is an escape valve for the pressures of life... [but] loud, inappropriate laughter will offend the Spirit.

It's interesting that he said a good sense of humor helps revelation. "You want to be more inspired? Develop your sense of humor!" Is he really saying humor is a divine attribute? I think so. President Hinckley had a great sense of humor, if you remember, and so does President Monson. Although this may seem out of character, I can even imagine the Savior grinning at a wholesome joke. I'm sure he's had a few good laughs at me, or with me, over the years. The trick, then, is to measure yourself and figure out if you need more of the godly kind of humor, or whether your laughter is too much and too loud. Either way, more holiness is the goal.

Now, back to what the gospel teaches us about how to be holy.

Elder Scott said this in that same sermon, which is modern scripture: "[Spirituality] can be enhanced by good health practices. Exercise, reasonable amounts of sleep, and good eating habits increase our capacity to receive

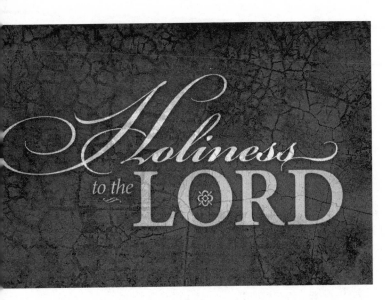

Holiness to the LORD

and understand revelation... We can improve both the quality of our service and our well-being by making careful, appropriate choices." So even our diet, our bedtime, and how often we exercise are part of holiness—holiness means taking care of our whole soul, body and spirit. *The Savior did* when he walked the mortal earth: When he was a boy he focused on perfection in four areas: "[1] wisdom... [2] stature... [3] favour with God, and [4] [favor with] man" (Luke 2:52). I like to think of these as mental, physical, spiritual, and emotional fitness. But I'm straying again. My point here is just to emphasize that taking care of your body—physical fitness—is a holy thing to do.

Each of the standard works teaches us about becoming holy—about the purification process in giving up anything ungodly:

The Doctrine and Covenants invites us to "cease from all your light speeches, from all laughter, from all your lustful desires, from all your pride and light-mindedness, and from all your wicked doings" (D&C 88:121).

The New Testament warns us that unholy attributes will become commonplace right before Christ returns: "Men shall be lovers of their own selves, covetous, boasters, proud, blasphemers, disobedient to parents, unthankful, unholy" (2 Timothy 3:2). These are all things we need to give up or steer clear of.

The Old Testament teaches us to "put difference between holy and unholy, and between unclean and clean" (Leviticus 10:10). In other words, put *distance* between you and those things. So to be holy means to be separate.

And *The Book of Mormon* says that "the Spirit of the Lord doth not dwell in unholy temples" (Helaman 4:24).

As you know, Grandpa was a patriarch in our stake not long ago. As part of that calling, he had to be extremely in-tune with the Spirit so he could receive revelation for the people he was blessing. He gave up just about all popular media, including most types of movies, music, and books, and he did it to invite the Spirit to be with him more fully. I've always thought about how hard that would be, but I believe when he did that he took several big steps on the stairs of holiness.

Because you have so many older siblings, you know that missionaries also distance themselves from those things while they're serving. So plan on it. It's a big sacrifice, but isn't the added measure of the Spirit a worthy reward—one that's worth more than what was given up? The truth is, I haven't yet mustered the devotion it takes to do this in my regular life, not wholly. I've given up some but not all. This brings us back to the discussion we had on being fully devoted—like the albino assassin—and there I go, drawing on the temporal for my inspiration. I guess it's a battle I'm not fit to win. Not yet. But I'll keep trying, and I hope you will too.

And until we gain the full victory, let's keep singing: "More holiness give me—more strivings within."

33. CHASTITY

This covenant is an important one too.

First off, Alma told his son Corianton, who had just messed up, that breaking the law of chastity was "most abominable above all sins save it be the shedding of innocent blood or denying the Holy Ghost" (Alma 39:5). In other words, on God's bottom-ten, this is number three—the third worst. Elder Jeffrey R. Holland explained why: "Clearly among [God's] greatest concerns regarding mortality are how one gets into this world and how one gets out of it" ("Personal Purity"). It's a serious sin because it can't be repaired or undone—not through any earthly means. (Fortunately for us, Christ has the divine power to undo both sin and death.)

Now remember, this isn't a rule because God wants to be arbitrary and mean—it's not for his sake at all. He made the law as a railing that will keep us from wrecking our lives. He wants to keep us from self-destructively obscuring the pathway to happiness. He's simply teaching us to live the good life.

Jeff, you and I are blessed to be part of an exemplary family, including our extended family. So we know first hand how awesome it can be—to have that support, friendship, and love. Having a loyal family really is the pathway to happiness. This fact will hit home even stronger when you're a missionary and you see the bad things that happen when the family fortress has fallen. (Sorry. I should watch out for those apostolic alliterations, but, I promise, it just came out that way.)

And because family is a true principle, God gave us the law of chastity—so we know how to be happy: "Thou shalt love thy wife with all thy heart, and shalt cleave unto her and none else. And he that looketh upon a woman to lust after her shall deny the faith, and shall not have the Spirit; and if he repents not he shall be cast out" (D&C 42:22-23). That's a big deal, by the way—if you break this law, the Spirit won't be with you.

The proclamation on the family describes the law of chastity like this:

> The first commandment that God gave to Adam and Eve pertained to their potential for parenthood as husband and wife. We declare that God's commandment for His children to multiply and replenish the earth remains in force. We further declare that God has commanded that the sacred powers of procreation are to be employed only between man and woman, lawfully wedded as husband and wife. We declare the means by which mortal life is created to be divinely appointed. We affirm the sanctity of life and of its importance in God's eternal plan.

That paragraph is packed with doctrine. But the gist is that until you get legally married you have to be celibate, which, to be brutally honest, is a difficult thing to do when you're single and approaching thirty. As a slight tangent, I'd guess it's pretty difficult for someone struggling with same gender attraction too. But that doesn't make it any less important—the path to happiness is clear. It's the path of holiness.

President Ezra Taft Benson said, "The decision to be chaste and virtuous need only be made once. Make that decision now and let it be so firm and with such deep commitment that it can never be shaken... Decide now!" ("The Law of Chastity," given at BYU in 1987). In that same speech he said, "The first seeds of immorality are always sown in the mind," which makes it all the more important to fill our minds with holy things and to keep the unclean out. President Packer suggested that singing a hymn can be a powerful way to invite the Spirit back onto your mind's stage (and you know I'm a big fan of battle songs).

The adversary—the father of lies, the one who wants Christ's soldiers to fail in their wandering quests—uses a lot of the most popular media to cover up truth. He wants us to believe sexual pleasures are natural and acceptably gratified. But C. S. Lewis explained,

> This association is a lie. Like all powerful lies, it is based on a truth—the truth... is that sex in itself (apart from the excess and obsessions that have grown round it) is "normal" and "healthy"... The lie consists in the suggestion that any sexual act to which you are tempted at the moment is also healthy and normal. (*Mere Christianity* 92)

That brings us back to the battle against mistruth: What

this issue boils down to is that God has taught us the truth about how to be happy.

Now, in case anyone reading this may have started to despair, that isn't the point. To Corianton, and to anyone else who has slipped up in this area, the Lord is a talented enough physician to still save you: "Though [your sins] be red like crimson," he said, "they shall be [white] as wool" (Isaiah 1:18).

I would leave our discussion on chastity alone after that, but a couple of things are still unsaid. Luckily, C. S. Lewis and Jeffrey R. Holland make one of most powerful tag-teams that ever stepped into the ring. I'll let them take it from here, Lewis first:

> The Christian idea of marriage is based on Christ's words that a man and wife are to be regarded as <u>a single organism</u>—for that is what the words "one flesh" would be in modern English. And the Christians believe that, when He said this, He was not expressing a sentiment but stating a fact—just as one is stating a fact when one says that <u>a lock and its key are one mechanism,</u> or that a violin and a bow are one musical instrument. The inventor of the human machine was telling us that its two halves, the male and the female, were made to be combined together in pairs. (*Mere Christianity* 95)

He's teaching us *how* marriage can bless us—through unification. Elder Holland then adds this:

> From the Garden of Eden onward, marriage was intended to mean <u>the complete merger of a man and a</u>

woman—their hearts, hopes, lives, love, family, future, everything. Adam said of Eve that she was bone of his bones and flesh of his flesh, and that they were to be "one flesh" in their life together. This is a union of such completeness that we use the word *seal* to convey its eternal promise. The Prophet Joseph Smith once said we perhaps could render such a sacred bond as being "welded" one to another. ("Personal Purity")

Elder Holland continues with a lengthy passage I just can't leave out because it teaches *why* this is the way to happiness:

One aspect of that divinity given to virtually all men and women is the use of His power to create a human body, that wonder of all wonders—a genetically and spiritually unique being never before seen in the history of the world and never to be duplicated again in all the ages of eternity. A child, your child—with eyes and ears and fingers and toes and a future of unspeakable grandeur. Probably only a parent who has held that newborn infant in his or her arms understands the wonder of which I speak. Suffice it to say that of all the titles God has chosen for Himself, Father is the one He favors most, and *creation* is His watchword—especially human creation, creation in His image. You and I have been given something of that godliness, but under the most serious and sacred of restrictions. [Because he regards our agency so highly,] the only control placed on us is self-control—self-control born of respect for the divine sacramental power this gift represents.

I love this passage because it praises humans so highly. And by the same token, it honors the power by which humans appear on mortal turf—romantic love. It's the means by which God's children begin their sojourn.

Romantic love has at least one other important purpose. It's a special kind of love that teaches us about the highest type of love:

> As nature, for the nature-lover, gives a content to the word *glory*, so this [romantic love] gives a content to the word *Charity*. It is as if Christ said to us through [romantic love], "Thus—just like this—with this prodigality—not counting the cost—you are to love me and the least of my brethren." (C. S. Lewis, *The Four Loves* 110)

So he's saying that when we fall head-over-heels for someone, when we're so far gone we'll do almost anything for even a glimpse of their smile—that's the same devotion we ought to have toward God and toward the rest of his children. It gives us a simple way to experience something that's otherwise very difficult to encounter. Romantic love teaches godly love.

Now, as we move on to the next commandment, I want to point out how these build on each other:

You have to be obedient in order to make sacrifices.

You have to make sacrifices in order to become holy.

You have to be holy in order to have a godly marriage.

And you have to learn godly love through marriage if you're going to complete the last of these commandments.

34. CONSECRATION

Consecrate comes from Latin meaning "together + sacred" (*com + sacrare*). So *to consecrate* is to unite something with the sacred. It's the opposite of *desecrate*, which is to make a *holy* thing *unholy*—or take a sacred thing *away* from the sacred (remember the minstrel boy's harp).

In our church, an elder will take olive oil, which is just a regular old food (aside from its symbolism), and consecrate it to be used in anointings, meaning from then on it will only be used for sacred purposes—not food anymore.

One of God's laws is called the law of consecration. It's been practiced on occasion throughout the ages: The people of Enoch were called *Zion*, "because they were of one heart and one mind, and dwelt in righteousness; and there was no poor among them" (Moses 7:18). The saints in the holy land, directly after the Savior left, united themselves in the same way: "All that believed were together, and had all things common; and sold their possessions and goods, and parted them to all men, as every man had need" (Acts 2:44-55). After the Savior visited the ancient-American saints, they started doing the same thing: "They had all things common among them; therefore there were not rich and poor, bond and free, but they were all made free, and partakers of the heavenly gift" (4 Nephi 1:3). The Lord instructed the latter-day saints to live this law too in D&C 42:30-39, if you want to read about it.

So, according to these verses, *consecration* means giving the stuff we own into a community pool. That's true—and being willing to do this is part of how we can live this law now. But it's more than that:

The law of consecration is a divine principle whereby men and women voluntarily dedicate their <u>time, talents, and material wealth</u> to the establishment and building up of God's kingdom. ("The Guide to the Scriptures")

So it's more than just our material possessions. It's our time too. And our talents. It's giving more than our things—it's giving ourselves. And we're not just giving it to a random community—we're giving it to build up the kingdom of God.

The greatest commandment is to love God with your heart, might, mind, and strength. In other words, with everything you've got—your whole *being*. That's what charity is—to have that perfect devotion to God. Consecration seems to simply be the physical manifestation of that charitable, godly-love state of mind.

Also, charity naturally bleeds out—if we really love God with our whole being, the consequence is that we love his children too—as much as ourselves (the second greatest commandment). When we reach that point, we love those around us just as much as we love ourselves, which lets us become one. The Lord told us to "be one; and if ye are not one ye are not mine" (D&C 38:27). We'll then have no unkind feelings for anyone else. "Therefore if thou bring thy gift to the altar, and there rememberest that thy brother hath ought against thee; Leave there thy gift before the altar, and go thy way; first be reconciled to thy brother, and then come and offer thy gift" (Matt 5:23-24).

The law of consecration helps us, knights errant, to prove ourselves all the more, and it requires the sharpening of the previous laws—we have to sacrifice so much, we have to set apart our labors as holy, and we have to love unconditionally. "And Zion cannot be built up unless it is by the principles of [this] law of the celestial kingdom; otherwise I cannot receive her unto myself" (D&C 105:5). So a celestial world functions this way, where the needs of your friends and your neighbors are just as important as your own. The Savior said we should "Love one another... as I have loved you" (John 13:34)—love as much as he loved, and he loved a lot—enough to suffer an infinite depth on our behalf and then die for us too. That's how much we're supposed to love other people.

Just like I can't enter "the place of no thorns" if I'm carrying a thorn, I can't dwell in the place of perfection if I can't live the law there—I have to meet the conditions of the place.

This isn't so easy either. This law, I think, is the heaviest one by far—a huge sacrifice. But, again, the returns will be greater than what we give up. The Lord said, "And thus I grant unto this people a privilege of organizing themselves according to my laws" (D&C 51:15), which is a cool way to think about it—it's a privilege.

He went on to say that "whoso is found a faithful, a just, and a wise steward shall enter into the joy of his Lord, and shall inherit eternal life" (D&C 51:19). Our dad—the accountant—has talked to us on occasion about keeping our finances in order. One of the ideas he likes to emphasize is *stewardship*: Everything we have in life, including whatever financial success we achieve, is a gift from God. And we should never start thinking that they belong to us or that we have the right to keep them from our fellowmen. Maybe that's why the Lord said this:

> If any man shall take of the abundance which I have made, and impart not his portion, according to the law of my gospel, unto the poor and the needy, he shall, with the wicked, lift up his eyes in hell, being in torment. (D&C 104:18)

This alludes to the parable Christ taught many years before about the rich man and Lazarus the beggar (which you can read in Luke 16:19-31). It reminds me of a quote I love from C. S. Lewis:

> I do not believe one can settle how much we ought to give. I am afraid <u>the only safe rule is to give more than we can spare</u>. In other words, if our expenditure on comforts, luxuries, amusements, etc., is up to the standard common among those with the same income as our own, we are probably giving away too little. If our charities do not at all pinch or hamper us, I should say they are too small. There ought to be things we should like to do and cannot do because our charitable expenditure excludes them. (*Mere Christianity* 81)

Wow—"more than we can spare." That's a lot. It's a rough rule. The *last* rule in a lot of ways—one that lets us prove our mettle.

It wouldn't be so hard if we were giving the money or the time directly to Christ—not after what he did for us. It might even seem like a trifling way to return the favor, almost an insult because it's so small in comparison. Along those same lines, he taught us this: "Inasmuch as ye have done it unto one of the least of these my brethren, ye have done it unto me" (Matthew 25:40). And ultimately, when we give our lives to serve others, we're giving them to build Christ's kingdom—it's a battle won for Christendom. But we, as the victors, get our share of the spoils: It changes our insides—changes our very being.

Temples give us the template to build a perfect society, which, with God's help, we can build, just like Enoch and his people did. They built a city called "the City of Holiness, even Zion. And... Enoch talked with the Lord... [who] showed unto Enoch all the inhabitants of the earth; and... in process of time, [Zion] was taken up into heaven" (Moses 7:18-21). After learning to truly live the celestial law, including the law of consecration, in their actions as well as in their hearts, they finished their sojourn, and returned to their true home.

35. O Remember

I had ACL surgery a few years back, which left me bed-ridden for a whole week. When I tried to stand on my right leg again, I was surprised by how quickly and thoroughly my muscle had atrophied. While sitting in a chair, it was basically impossible to even raise my foot into the air—and this weakness had come in only one short week! But that's how mortality works. Everything naturally atrophies—our minds, I think, most of all. But there's a sure way to safeguard against atrophy—we just have to keep using the muscle. Once isn't enough. Instead, consistency is key—repeating and re-strengthening steadily, slow and steady, drip by drip.

We've covered a lot so far, more than you can probably remember. And there's still more. Which brings up an important point: If we go home and don't *remember* the covenants we made in the temple—and if we don't strive to keep them—then none of it really matters. What you learned will quickly atrophy.

I came up with a mnemonic model, structured around my fist, as a way to remember the parts of the endowment. I'm not going to explain it here, but I included it anyway because it looks like something you'd find in "dad's grail diary." The point, though, is just that remembering is important—with the covenants in particular.

In Alma's awesome sermon to the people in Zarahemla, he asked them if they had *"sufficiently* retained in remembrance" how God had delivered them and how he would again later. In other words, he was asking, "Have you remembered *enough?"* This echoes that idea of being *more* devoted—achieving higher levels of commitment through remembering *more*.

Wearing the garment is one helpful reminder, as long as we don't forget it's something special (which is tough, since it's an every-day item).

The Lord had a way of reminding the ancient Israelites, which he told to Moses:

> Speak unto the children of Israel, and bid them that they make them fringes in the borders of their garments throughout their generations, and that they put upon the fringe of the borders a ribband of blue...

<u>that ye may look upon it, and remember</u> all the commandments of the Lord, and do them; and that ye <u>seek not after your own heart</u> and your own eyes... That ye may remember, and do all my commandments, <u>and be holy</u> unto your God. I am the Lord your God, which brought you out of the land of Egypt. (Numbers 15:37-41)

Here's a funny story (if you'll excuse another tangent). On my mission, I read *The Book of Mormon*, *The New Testament*, *The Doctrine and Covenants*, and *The Pearl of Great Price*. Then I got ready to read *The Old Testament* for the first time ever. I calculated how many pages per day I'd need to read in order to finish in a reasonable timeframe and got started right away. Soon I was halfway through Exodus. Now, you may not know, but on a mission, your zone will meet with your president in a conference every six weeks (a "transfer"). He'll instruct the whole group of

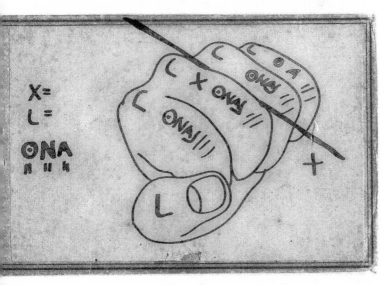

missionaries, but he'll also take time to interview everyone individually. So in my zone conference interview, I eagerly told President Booth about my goal to read *The Old Testament* for the first time. And he said, "Elder, there are better ways for you to spend your study time."

That surprised me a little, but I obeyed anyway (and I honestly wasn't too sad to not have to wade through Leviticus—Elder Niederhauser had warned me). But because of that interview, I went my whole mission, two years of discussing Christian doctrine with dozens of strangers, and I'd never even read the whole Bible. Kind of ironic. But it allowed me to focus on more foundational matters, which was definitely good—I feel confident President Booth's advice was inspired. So it wasn't until several years after my mission that I returned to that goal. In June of 2011, I finally finished *The Old Testament*. And I mined quite a few gems out of it as I did.

This story was the long way around, but I just wanted to highlight the coolness of that last scripture I quoted—which I discovered by reading from cover to cover. (There are tons of these gems in there, by the way; they just don't come at the same frequency as in other scriptures.) What a message: "Seek not after your own heart and your own eyes... and be holy." It's beautiful. And it's a message worth remembering.

And that brings it back: The point is that we need to remember—whether your method is like mine or like the ancient Israelites (probably you'll have an even better way). Our mortal memories naturally fade, and so do our resolves—like an atrophying muscle. But we can fight these natural tendencies if we stay consistent.

36. Clothed As Priests

When I was in London, I ditched my classmates and the travel-buddy rule. Because I had a mission:

I had to find Herbert Johnson Hatters at 54 Saint James's Street.

I wasn't sure my peers would understand, so I'd slipped out rather than explain: Herbert Johnson was the milliner who made the original Indiana Jones fedora and sold it to Steven Spielberg back in 1980.

After jogging through crowds, darting through traffic, and making a few wrong turns, I found myself at a doorway with a golden 54 displayed on the maroon background overhead. I walked inside the small shop and glanced around the shelves, breathing heavily from my run. A clerk approached and asked if he could help me. I humbly explained my quest, and a moment later he handed the fedora to me. I moved in front of a mirror and saw *me*—standing in blue jeans, a dark T-shirt, and an orange backpack. I pinched the hat's front crown in my fingers and put it on my head. And I couldn't help but grin. It was a big grin too, which was embarrassing, since the clerk was still watching. I wiped my smile away and took the hat off, asking him how much it was. He said a hundred and fifty quid—which meant £150. That was nearly $300 in American money. Too much for me to actually buy it, but that wasn't entirely unexpected. I asked for his card and told him I might have him ship it to the states. (Which was true—and I still might, if people find this book worthwhile.)

When I stepped out of that store, I felt like I could do anything—like adventure was in the very air, and all I had to do was breathe it in. And I wasn't even wearing the hat anymore. It didn't matter though—I was still wearing it in my mind's mirror. And that image of myself, that version of me, could dare any height or confront any evil. It's funny that such a little thing could have such a big effect on how I felt. But it did.

It's a small example of how the way we dress impacts what we think. That's why, before we begin the endowment, we change from street clothes into white clothes. The workers there are dressed in white too. Because we've already talked about "putting on Christ" and *holiness* and *sanctification*, you know what this symbolizes. When Alma taught about the righteous saints, he said, "They were called after [Christ's] holy order, and were sanctified, and their garments were washed white through the blood of the Lamb" (Alma 13:11). To get into heaven, you don't actually need white clothing. It's just a symbol. But it represents the cleanliness of the soul, which *is* important. It also helps to unify everyone there—soldiers wearing the same Christian uniform.

As I've mentioned, the modern temple ceremony *isn't* the exact same one the wandering Israelites performed. But they're definitely similar. So let's dig just a bit deeper into *The Old Testament*—so you at least have an idea of what to expect when you go to the temple. Here's what the high priest wore when he entered the portable tabernacle or the temple at Jerusalem:

> And he put upon him the <u>coat</u>, and girded him with the <u>girdle</u>, and clothed him with the <u>robe</u>, and put the <u>ephod</u> upon him, and he girded him with the

curious girdle of the ephod, and bound it unto him therewith. And he put the <u>breastplate</u> upon him: also he put in the breastplate the Urim and the Thummim. And he put the <u>mitre</u> upon his head; also upon the mitre, even upon his forefront, did he put the golden plate, the <u>holy crown</u>; as the Lord commanded Moses. (Leviticus 8:6-9)

One thing you'll notice, he did "as the Lord commanded." God instructed him to do things a certain way, and he obeyed.

The same holy clothing is mentioned earlier in Exodus:

Thou shalt make holy garments for Aaron thy brother <u>for glory and for beauty</u>. And thou shalt speak unto... <u>whom I have filled with the spirit of wisdom</u>, that they may make Aaron's garments <u>to consecrate him, that he may minister unto me in the priest's office</u>. And these are the garments which they shall make; a breastplate, and an ephod, and a robe, and a broidered coat, a mitre, and a girdle. (Exodus 28:2-4)

This next picture shows the high priest wearing the clothing just mentioned. We're going to look at each piece individually—starting at the top, and going from outside to inside (the reverse order the priest would put them on).

Mitre

Mitre is an English word, which we already discussed. The Hebrews called this headdress a *mitznefet*. It was "wound around the head so as to form a broad, flat-topped turban." All the priests wore this. The one the high priest wore had a special golden diadem (a plate of solid gold) with

Mitre

Breastplate

Girdle

Ephod

Incense

Robe

Under-tunic

these words etched into it: קדש ליהוה (*Wikipedia*, "Mitre," see Exodus 39:14, 39:30).

> The high priest [alone] wore a golden band on the front of his mitre on the forehead. Engraved on the band were the words "Holiness to the Lord," <u>signifying first that the high priest should be characterized by this attribute [of holiness]</u>, and <u>second that Christ, the Great High Priest, would be perfectly holy before God</u>. (*Old Testament Student Manual* 153; see Exodus 28:36-39)

So the mitre meant the wearer was holy—which made him, in that way, like Christ. Putting those words to his forehead adds to the symbol as well—that the mind itself is affected. Here are those words again, in an elegant font, which you read from right to left:

Breastplate

The high priest wore one other thing (along with the golden diadem) that the regular priests didn't: a fabric breastplate fastened by golden chains (Exodus 28:13-30). It was a square with 12 precious stones set into it. The names of the 12 tribes were etched into these stones.

As a side note, the high priest was the only one allowed to traverse the veil into the Holy of Holies, and he got to do this just once a year. But the moment Christ died, the ensuing storms ripped down the temple veil (Matthew 27:51). This may have symbolized that now, because of Christ's atonement, all men had access to the mercy seat—or the infinite goodness of God.

Girdle or Sash

The priests also wore a sash (called an *avnet* in Hebrew) made of white linen, and its purpose was "for glory and for beauty" (Exodus 28:41). The high priest's was a little fancier—an "embroidered work" of blue, purple, and scarlet (Exodus 28:39, 39:29).

Ephod or Apron

The *Old Testament Student Manual* explains the *ephod* pretty thoroughly, so I'll let it do the talking:

> The Lord directed that <u>they were not to wear ordinary clothing during their service</u>, but they were to have "holy garments" made by those whom the Lord had "filled with the spirit of wisdom" (Exodus 28:2-3). These sacred garments were to be passed from father to son along with the high priestly office itself (Exodus 29:29). The ephod, worn over a blue robe, was made of blue, purple, and scarlet material, with designs of gold thread skillfully woven into the fabric... The exact function of the ephod is not known. As President Joseph Fielding Smith observed, information concerning these ancient ordinances "was <u>never recorded</u> in any detail because <u>such ordinances are sacred and not for the world</u>..." This "apron," as it is sometimes translated, signified a beautiful symbolic concept. With the two onyx stones, which fastened the ephod

on the shoulders, the high priest (<u>a type of Christ and also of His authorized representatives</u>) entered the tabernacle (the house of the Lord, or God's presence) <u>carrying Israel on his shoulders</u> (see Exodus 28:12). (*Old Testament Student Manual* 152)

Robe or Tunic

The priests wore a robe called a *ketonet*. It was made from pure linen and covered the body from the neck to the wrists and down to the ankles. The Jewish Talmud teaches that "the wearing of the *ketonet* atoned for the sin of bloodshed on the part of the Children of Israel" (*Wikipedia*, "Priestly tunic").

> This robe... was <u>woven without seams</u>... (see Exodus 28:31–32). Jesus, the Great High Priest, was clothed in a similar seamless garment prior to His Crucifixion (see John 19:23)... "[It] set forth <u>the idea of wholeness or spiritual integrity</u>; and the dark-blue colour indicated nothing more than the heavenly origin and character of the office with which the robe was associated..." (*Old Testament Student Manual* 152)

Under Tunic

The underwear—the first things the priest put on—were fully covered by the robe. They were called the *michnasayim* and were also made of pure linen. With the other clothing, there was a plain version for the priests and a more intricate version for the high priest. But with these, they both wore the same style. And instead of being for beauty, these were for modesty, "to cover the flesh of their nakedness" (Exodus 28:42). According to the Talmud,

"The *michnasayim* symbolized the abolition of the distinction between the heavenly and the mortal part of man" (*Wikipedia*, "Priestly undergarments"). In other words, there's no difference between your physical body and your spiritual soul—they're united as one and must be made holy together.

Summary

So, as a quick wrap-up: The under tunic was like underwear. The priest covered this with a robe that went all the way to his ankles. On top of the robe was an ephod—an intricate apron. Over that he tied an embroidered sash. And on his head he wore the holy crown. This clothing symbolically raised the priests higher than their regular mortal selves, helping them remember their truer nature and their eternal purpose as children of God. The outfit could symbolize the uniform of a Christian soldier. It also has (perhaps stronger) ties to that of royalty—the attire of a kingly priest.

37. PASSING THE ANGEL SENTINELS

This next quote seems to me like it's straight out of an epic like *Paradise Lost*. If I let my imagination run a little wild, I see the angels towering overhead, with their wings (yes, I imagine wings) stretching skyward, their gauntleted hands resting on the pommels of their burning swords as they glare, as if daring any unworthy traveler to pass through the way of life:

Your endowment is to receive all those ordinances in

the house of the Lord which are necessary for you, after you have departed this life, to enable you to walk back to the presence of the Father, passing the angels who stand as sentinels, being enabled to give them the key words, the signs and tokens, pertaining to the holy Priesthood, and gain your eternal exaltation in spite of earth and hell. (*Discourses of Brigham Young* 416)

Now I want you to go back and re-read that because there's more to it than just the imagery. But I'm not going to explain or expound (I'll even leave the underlining up to you this time).

The *Pearl of Great Price Student Manual* tells the story of the Joseph Smith papyri (and it's worth reading the whole chapter on The Book of Abraham). The short version, though, is that Joseph acquired some fragmented Egyptian scrolls, several of which became the basis for The Book of Abraham. For fun or for "dad's grail diary," I've included a scan of one of the few pieces of these scrolls that survived (after Joseph's death they passed from one proprietor to another till eventually most of them were burned in the Chicago fire of 1871). This one is called "Joseph Smith Papyrus Segment IV."

Chapter 162 of *The Book of the Dead* explains that a soul who was properly prepared would cross that border into the eternal, where "his throne is surrounded by a flaming host. He will be a god in the land of the gods. He will not be turned back at any gate. This formula is tested and proven" (Hugh Nibley, "Three Facsimiles"). What Brigham Young taught us in that quote is the same thing the ancient

Egyptians sought—the right to traverse the passageway into eternity. They fully believed in apotheosis.

Joseph wanted three images from the papyri to be printed in *The Pearl of Great Price*, so he commissioned an artist to carve the same designs into wooden printer's blocks to be used at the press (the artist also filled in the gaps so the facsimiles would appear complete). I want to talk about Facsimile 2 in particular (the circle one). It's something called a *hypocephalus*—and you'll find similar ones in places like the British Museum (though no two are exactly alike). Because the ancient Egyptians were obsessed with death, or rather, with not having to die—at least not permanently—they would place a hypocephalus, often made of precious metal, behind the head of a corpse as a ritualistic way of pointing the deceased toward eternal life. These *hypocephalus* designs also come from *The Book of the Dead*, and, as Wikipedia says,

> The scenes portrayed on them relate to... resurrection and life after death, connecting them with the Osirian myth... The daily setting and rising of the sun was a symbol of death and rebirth. The hypocephalus represented all that the sun encircles—the world of the living, over which it passed during the day, was depicted in the upper half, and that of the dead, which it crossed during the night, in the lower portion. ("Hypocephalus")

To the Egyptians, this disc was a spell—a series of words, an ordered story—that would "cause the head and body to be enveloped in flames of radiance, making the deceased divine" (*FairMormon.org*, "Facsimile 2"). So you say the

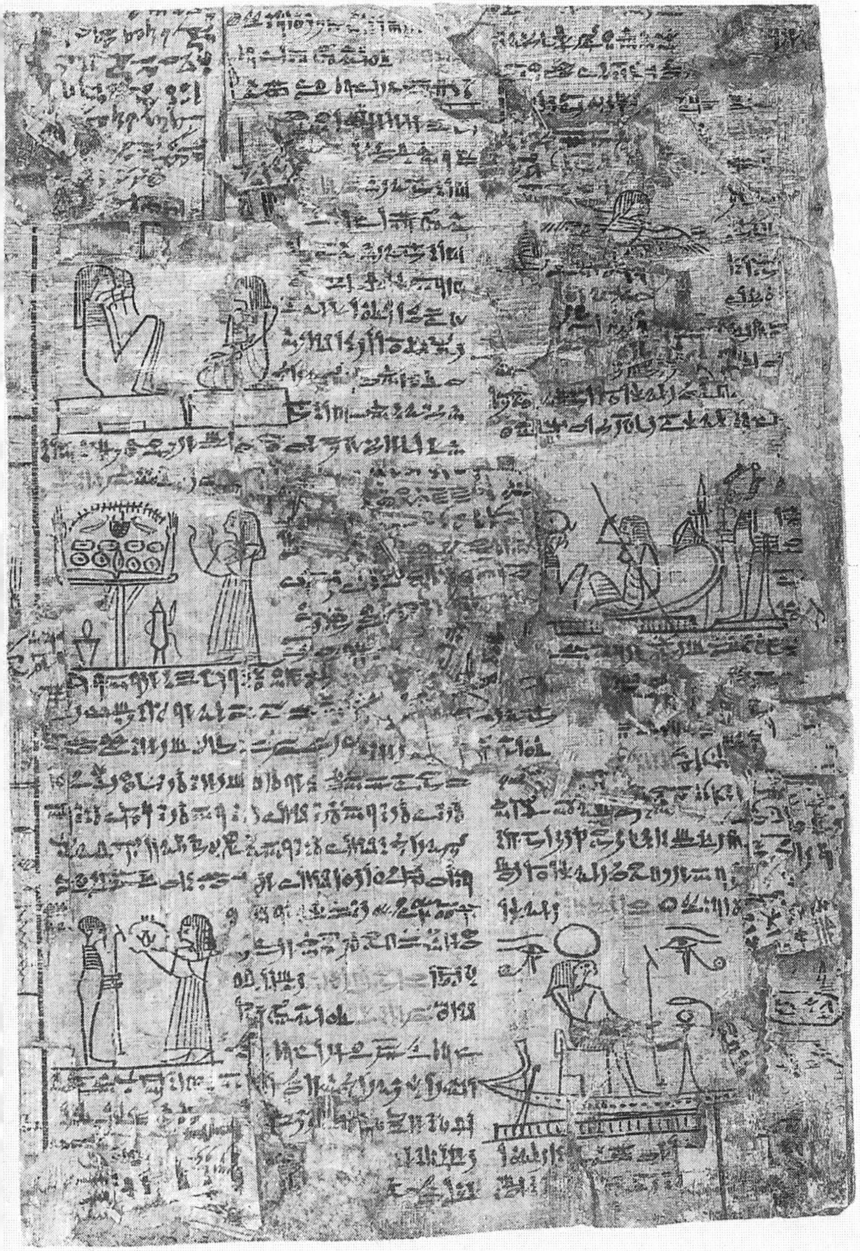

right words, and when you die you cross into eternity. Whether that worked for the Egyptians, we've yet to see, but the concept is majestic. It assured "deliverance from the destroyer and resurrection to the person lying helpless on the altar under the blackness of death" (Nibley). In other words, it was their way of getting past those angel sentinels in the hereafter so they could enter the way of life.

Here is Facsimile 2 (in this version, the dark splotch that covers much of the upper right represents the missing parts that were filled in by the artist):

I want to highlight a couple pieces from Joseph's annotations of this facsimile (which you'll find in the scriptures right next to it):

> 3. Is made to represent God, sitting upon his throne, clothed with power and authority; with a crown of eternal light upon his head; representing also the grand Key-words of the Holy Priesthood, as revealed to Adam in the Garden of Eden, as also to Seth, Noah, Melchizedek, Abraham, and all to whom the Priesthood was revealed...

> 7. Represents God sitting upon his throne, revealing through the heavens the grand Key-words of the Priesthood; as, also, the sign of the Holy Ghost unto Abraham, in the form of a dove.

> 8. Contains writings that cannot be revealed unto the world; but is to be had in the Holy Temple of God.

> 9. Ought not to be revealed at the present time.

I'm trying to teach you about one of the most sacred parts of the temple ceremony, but because it's most sacred, I don't think I should speak more directly than this. I apologize for that. But I've laid it out for you to think about. And even if I don't give you all the answers here, it will be helpful for you to arrive at the temple with the right *questions*.

What the Egyptians wanted so badly was what Enoch and a whole city figured out—how to live a godly life and become worthy to enter the presence of God. The gospel of Christ promises to teach us this same thing. Christ himself faced death, and he came off conqueror—defeating that enemy the Egyptians feared. And people witnessed his victory: "He rose again the third day according to the scriptures: And... was seen of Cephas, then of the twelve: After that, he was seen of above five hundred brethren at once; of whom the greater part remain unto this present, but some are fallen asleep" (1 Corinthians 15:4-6). And now that he has conquered, he offers that gift to us.

This is the great work we're pursuing, to be exalted and brought back into the presence of our Father in Heaven, where, as Edward Partridge wrote, we'll "meet the Lord and Enoch's band triumphant in the air" ("Let Zion in Her Beauty Rise").

38. PRAYER

Jeff, with your permission, I'd like to tell a story about you.

Your night terrors were bad when you were little. I can only speculate about how scary they were to you. But to me, as an onlooker, they were pretty frightening. Even though you *weren't* awake, you *seemed* awake in every way. You'd be standing up with your eyes open, pointing and looking at something horrifying. And your expression was so genuine that I would look too, as if I might see the phantom that was haunting you. Of course, there was never anything there—not that I could see anyway. And it was difficult to calm you down and back to sleep.

One evening (when you were awake), you told me how bad it was to face the night, again and again, and I had the thought to share a scripture with you:

Counsel with the Lord in all thy doings, and he will direct thee for good; yea, when thou liest down at night lie down unto the Lord, that he may watch over you in your sleep; and when thou risest in the morning let thy heart be full of thanks unto God; and if ye do these things, ye shall be lifted up at the last day. (Alma 37:37)

You must have really taken that scripture to heart that night—but I can't tell your part of the story, just mine. You came to me later and thanked me, and you were fighting not to cry as you told me that it had made a difference. You were just a little kid, but I was struck by the thought that you *knew* through personal experience that it really worked—that *he had* watched over you in your sleep. It was a powerful moment for me—to have such a young kid witness that he knew prayer was real.

Prayer is an important part of our mortal sojourn—and it's something everyone could stand to learn better. I love two aspects in particular of the Bible Dictionary's entry on prayer. First, it simply defines it:

Prayer is the act by which the <u>will of the Father and the will of the child are brought into correspondence</u> with each other. The object of prayer is not to change the will of God, but to secure for ourselves and for others blessings that God is already willing to grant, but that are made conditional on our asking for them.

You asked for peace that night, and God sent it. Through prayer, you accessed what God wanted for you. It's good to be reminded that prayer isn't about what we want (our will) but learning what our loving Father knows is best. It's about humility—we should go into it expecting ourselves to change, not God. In your case, God changed you by making you more sensitive to his Spirit, I suppose. But it should always be us, the children, who make the changes. Imagine a child arguing to his parents about a topic he doesn't even fully understand. The Lord said, "Enter ye in at the gate, as I have commanded, and seek not to counsel your God" (D&C 22:4). We need to learn to be submissive, to let go of our own stubborn ideas. It's a hard thing to do, but it's the goal.

The next part of the entry is also about the basic nature of prayer:

> As soon as we learn <u>the true relationship in which we stand toward God</u> (namely, God is our Father, and we are his children), then at once <u>prayer becomes natural and instinctive</u> on our part.

I love this. God is our Father—what an important truth. Jeff, you and I have an awesome dad, which makes it easy to understand the lovingkindness the word *father* embodies. It's pretty natural to ask Dad for advice—he has a lot of experience that you and I don't. In the same way, it's natural to go to our Father in Heaven.

The psalmist said, "My hands also will I lift up unto thy commandments, which I have loved; and I will meditate in thy statutes" (Psalm 119:48). I can see the poet clearly: with his whole soul, his mind and his "holy hands" as Timothy called them (1 Timothy 2:8), reaching for the heavens. And it uses the word *meditate*, which strikes me as a Buddhist word more than a Christian one (but it's actually used throughout the scriptures quite often)—suggesting that we ought to have frequent and focused thoughts about holier and higher things. This could be as intense as Enos's wrestle with God or as peaceful as "the doctrine of the priesthood [that] shall distil upon thy soul as the dews from heaven" (D&C 121:45).

Our world is as crazy-busy as a science fiction film—endlessly filled with memes, videos, and status updates. This static—meaningless noise—covers up the truer picture—the kingdom of God. On my mission, President Booth counseled us, his missionaries, to "find the mountaintop," which made a lasting impression on me—it's one of his lessons I think about most often. A mountain is the earthly place that is nearest to heaven.

When Nephi was ready to receive direction from the Lord, he heard a voice that said, "Arise, and get thee into the mountain" (1 Nephi 17:7). When he did, the Lord told him how to get to the promised land. Moses was "caught up into an exceedingly high mountain, [where] he saw God face to face, and he talked with him, and the glory of God was upon Moses; therefore Moses could endure his presence" (Moses 1:1-2). Moses then learned more about how man could act like God. The Savior took Peter, James, and John and "[brought] them up into an high mountain apart," which is one way of saying that this was a very exclusive event. When they were all alone up there, Christ "was transfigured before them: and his face did shine as the sun, and his raiment was white as the light" (Matthew 17:1-2). So they too had the privilege of seeing Christ in his glory—they beheld the face of God. And this, too, took place on a mountain, away from it all.

The message—the point of "find the mountaintop"—is embedded within these stories. Each shows a soldier of Christ leaving the place he usually spends his time and going on a hike to a high and excluded place. And it's in that special, now sacred, place that he "lift[s] up [his] hands toward [God's] holy oracle" (Psalms 28:2)—to commune with deity. That's what President Booth was trying to teach us—to make a habit of finding a quiet and solitary place to be alone with our Father. This is an important aspect of personal prayer and of receiving individualized revelation. I might add that while we ought to be seeking the mountaintop daily, the temple—the mountain of the Lord—is a particularly good place for this.

39. FAMILY PRAYER

The Lord specified that we should "establish a house... of prayer" (D&C 88:119). The temple is the ideal fulfillment of this—it's a house we enter to commune with our Father. And we don't just seek the Lord alone, but as united saints too—as a team and a family.

Elder Neal A. Maxwell said, "Among the transcendent things restored as a part of the 'restitution of all things' were... the initiatory ordinances, the holy endowment, <u>the true order of prayer</u>, baptism for the dead, [and] the sealing power" (*A Wonderful Flood of Light*). The *Encyclopedia of Mormonism* adds some detail about what that means for temple worship:

> The formation of <u>the prayer circle</u> suggests wholeness and eternity, and the participants, having affirmed

that they bear no negative feelings toward other members of the circle (see Matthew 5:23-24), evoke communal harmony in collective prayer—a harmony underscored by the linked formation, uniformity of dress, and the unison repetition of the words of the leader. The prayer has no set text, but is, among other things, an occasion for seeking the Lord's blessing upon those with particular needs <u>whose names have been submitted for collective entreaty</u>.

We've talked a bit about unity already. Enoch and his city were perfectly united. Christ taught us through his intercessory prayer that eternal life was to "know *thee* the only true God, and Jesus Christ, whom thou hast sent... That they all may be one; as thou, Father, art in me, and I in thee, that they also may be one in us" (John 17:3, 21). Exaltation includes *being one*, united with those around you—both God and your fellow men. To unite in prayer is a symbol that correlates with this idea.

Joseph Smith taught an object lesson on circles:

> I take my ring from my finger and liken it unto the mind of man—the immortal part, because it has no beginning. Suppose you cut it in two; then it has a beginning and an end; but join it again, and it continues one eternal round. So with the spirit of man... Intelligence is eternal and exists upon a self-existent principle. It is a spirit from age to age, and there is no creation about it. (*Teachings of the Prophet Joseph Smith*)

He was talking about the lifespan of a soul, but it applies

to everything that's eternal. As the hymn teaches, "There is no end to virtue; there is no end to might; there is no end to wisdom; there is no end to light" ("If You Could Hie to Kolob"). Next time you're sitting in church, you might flip to that hymn—it's whole point is centered around this concept of eternity—things that don't end—which includes our unification with God and our fellow man.

Let's go to *The Book of Mormon* for an example of unity in prayer: Zemnarihah became chief of the Gadianton robbers at a time when they were a massive force rather than a small secret brotherhood. He then laid siege to the rest of the outnumbered Nephites. So the Nephites prayed, and really meant it, and the Lord eventually granted them an escape. After he did, they rejoiced "<u>with one voice</u>, saying: May the God of Abraham, and the God of Isaac, and the God of Jacob, protect this people in righteousness, so long as they shall call on the name of their God..." And then they concluded by repeating his name: "Hosanna to the Most High God... Blessed be the name of the Lord God Almighty, the Most High God." (3 Nephi 4:30, 31).

In church, we pray as a group by having one person simply speak on behalf of the whole congregation. That's unity in prayer, but it's only metaphorically and not literally "with one voice." There are a few ways to literally speak in unison: First, you could say something that you've all memorized, which some churches do, but in ours we're a little wary of it becoming a "vain repetition" (Matthew 6:7, and, by the way, all memorized prayers are *not* vain—remember our sacrament). Second, you could have the Spirit inspire you to say the exact same words simultaneously, which I'm sure is possible but rare. Or, third, you could follow a leader by repeating the words he or she speaks. I would guess when the Nephites prayed with one voice they used this third method. When King Benjamin finished his legendary sermon, the people essentially made a promise to hearken. This they spoke

> with one voice, saying:... we believe all the words which thou hast spoken... we know of their surety and truth, because of the Spirit of the Lord Omnipotent, which has wrought a mighty change in us, or in our hearts, that we have no more disposition to do evil, but to do good continually. (Mosiah 5:2)

When the Savior came to the Nephites, he taught them to perform the sacrament. And after they had made that covenant, "They were filled with the Spirit; and they did cry out with one voice, and gave glory to Jesus" (3 Nephi 20:9). Again, this is a subtle detail that is easy to overlook—this speaking with one voice—but the implications seem obvious when you think about it. It's a way for a group to become more united by literally speaking as one.

To sum up, eternal life is to be one with God and with all our siblings, his children. This is a natural thing if we understand and respect the relationship we have with everyone involved. And this manifests itself through united prayer, which we do as families, wards, mission companions, spouses, and also as groups in the temple.

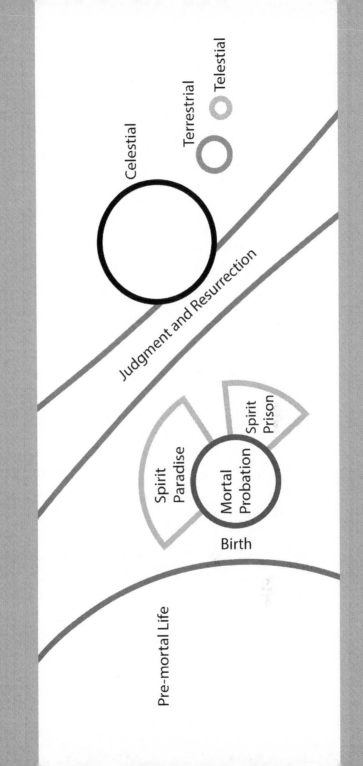

40. THE VEIL

We just barely talked about how Moses and Nephi approached the Lord on the mountaintop. They weren't the only ones.

Isaiah was one of Nephi's heroes. But Nephi didn't see heroic prophets as the only ones worthy to see the Lord. Nephi said, "[Isaiah] verily saw my Redeemer, even as I have seen him. And my brother, Jacob, also has seen him as I have seen him" (2 Nephi 11:2-3). So Nephi made himself worthy, just like his prophet hero, and then received that great blessing. I'm sure Nephi helped in raising Jacob too and in guiding him on the spiritual path, till he was worthy as well. No doubt their father, Lehi, was their primary guide and example. Each of them aspired to be worthy, and then, because of that, they saw the Lord.

The brother of Jared climbed Mount Shelem carrying sixteen regular old rocks. And when he got there, because he had enough faith, he saw the Lord too. And he had an interesting interview—a question and answer session: "Believest thou the words which I shall speak?" he was asked (Ether 3:11). He replied by bearing his testimony—proof that he was ready to learn more: "Yea, Lord, I know that thou speakest the truth, for thou art a God of truth, and canst not lie" (Ether 3:12). And then he was given deeper knowledge: "And when he had said these words, behold, the Lord showed himself unto him, and said: Because thou knowest these things ye are redeemed from the fall; therefore ye are brought back into my presence; therefore I show myself unto you" (Ether 3:13).

The temple symbolically mimics this same experience—a

mortal approaching the Lord. It's almost like a practice run. It is at least a solid reminder that we're not just biding our time here—we have a specific purpose, and that is to become worthy to approach the Lord and re-enter his presence. Let's not forget, either, that it is only through the miracles and mercies of Christ that we can ever be worthy. That's why taking his name on us, trying to be like him, and listening to his Spirit are so important.

TEMPORAL MATTERS: SCHEDULES

Once you receive your own endowment, you can return to do work for the deceased.

After arriving and changing into white clothes, here's the breakdown of how long each part takes (most people just do one of these each time they attend):

Initiatory   = 35 mins (5 names)
Endowment = 105 mins (1 name)
Sealings   = 60 mins (2 couples, 10 children)

If the temple is crowded, sometimes you have to wait before getting started too.

The bottleneck, as far as doing names goes, is the endowment—it takes the longest for a session and you only do one name at a time. So it's important to do lots of those. That said, if you're in a hurry, sometimes initiatory or sealings are a good way to go.

Also, some people get in a rut where they just do an endowment every time. It's actually a good idea to switch it up every once in awhile so you can be reminded of the full process—all the covenants and ordinances in the temple journey.

I explained the schedules because I like efficiency. But if there's any place you should put your watch aside and just be perfectly present, the temple is it. If you can, leave plenty of time in your temple schedule so you can enjoy the quiet meditation without worrying about temporal things.

41. Personal Study

Scripture

- Moses 2-4 (the creation, the garden, and the fall)

Sermons

- President David O. McKay's Temple Address
- "Invoking The Spirit of the Lord as Council Witness" by David E. Bokovoy

Extra Credit

- *An Egyptian Endowment* by Hugh Nibley
- "Three Facsimiles from The Book of Abraham" by Hugh Nibley
- "The Joseph Smith Hypocephalus: Twenty Years Later" by Michael D. Rhodes
- I also recommend the series of 11 short video clips from UCLA Professor of Egyptology Kerry Muhlestein. They're fun to watch and definitely the most accessible of any of these.

Go to jwashburn.com/books/dearjeff for links to these readings and a complete bibliography.

SEALING

I will lead thee by my hand, and I will take thee, to put upon thee my name, even the Priesthood of thy father, and my power shall be over thee.

— *Abraham 1:18*

42. THE CAPSTONE

Elder Packer said, "Temple marriage, that sealing ordinance, is a crowning blessing that you may claim in the holy temple" (*The Holy Temple*).

I want you to imagine the ordinances of the gospel as a pyramid. At the bottom you have faith, repentance, baptism, and the gift of the Holy Ghost. Those are the basics, right there. Above that you'd put faith, hope, and charity, I think—this is a rough analogy. Then maybe there would be the temple covenants, the ones we've reviewed so far. And then the very peak, the last triangle that becomes the capstone, is the sealing ordinance.

> In the celestial glory there are three heavens or degrees; and in order to obtain the highest, a man must enter into this order of the priesthood [meaning the new and everlasting covenant of marriage]; and if he does not, he cannot obtain it. He may enter into the other, but that is the end of his kingdom; he cannot have an increase. (D&C 131:1-4)

So it's the capstone because it's the gateway into the highest glory. But it's also the capstone because it's the conclusion, or that last item, in a larger work.

But Bruce R. McConkie described it this way: "All covenants between God and man are part of the new and everlasting covenant" (*Mormon Doctrine*, "New and Everlasting Covenant"). In other words, this last ordinance encompasses everything that came before it. It's a summation of the whole thing. So you might picture it like this instead—it being the whole pyramid:

New and Everlasting Covenant

It's not called a "new" covenant because it's going to blow your mind with new information. It's "new" because it's been made new with you:

> The gospel is the *everlasting* covenant because it is <u>ordained by Him who is Everlasting</u> and also because it is everlastingly the same. In all past ages salvation was gained by adherence to its terms and conditions, and that same compliance will bring the same reward in all future ages. <u>Each time this everlasting covenant is revealed it is new to those of that dispensation.</u> Hence the gospel is the new and everlasting covenant. (*Mormon Doctrine*, "New and Everlasting Covenant")

In that last sentence, he suggests that the entire gospel is the new and everlasting covenant. Interesting.

As I was thinking about the name of this covenant, I

came to this conclusion: The word *new* means the covenant promises *newness*. It's what the covenant is about—you're becoming a new self, born through Christ into a new and everlasting life. In the same way, it's called *everlasting* because it promises *everlastingness*. *Newness* and *everlastingness* are the qualities that the covenant is centered around. So it's the new and everlasting covenant.

After the creation, Adam and Eve were taught how to walk back to God—all the covenants that were necessary. That's the same covenant. And it's been taught from dispensation to dispensation from then until now. "This is a new and an everlasting covenant, even that which was from the beginning" (D&C 22:1). And the sealing ordinance that unites husband and wife with God is the conclusion.

(As a side note, I ought to mention that this isn't the end of all ordinances. There are at least a few others we mortals know about and probably many that we don't. But that's beyond the scope of our discussion here.)

43. THE PROMISES

In section 76, we learn about the three degrees of glory and the qualifications for each of them. It's a super important section.

It explains the highest glory like this:

> They are they into whose hands the Father <u>has given all things</u>—they are they who are <u>priests and kings</u>, who have received of his fulness, and of his glory; and are priests of the Most High, after the order of Melchizedek, which was after the order of Enoch,

which was <u>after the order of the Only Begotten Son</u>. Wherefore, as it is written, <u>they are gods, even the sons of God</u>—wherefore, <u>all things are theirs</u>, whether life or death, or things present, or things to come, all are theirs and they are Christ's, and Christ is God's. And they shall overcome all things. Wherefore, let no man glory in man, but rather let him glory in God, who shall subdue all enemies under his feet. (D&C 76:55-61)

This is a summation of all the promises the gospel has made, and they're wrapped up in that final sealing covenant which grants access to the highest glory. So this is what you should expect in that ordinance. Here they are as described in Joseph Smith's inspired prayer to dedicate the Kirtland temple:

> Remember all thy church, O Lord... That when the trump shall sound for the dead, we shall be caught up in the cloud to meet thee, that we may ever be with the Lord; <u>that our garments may be pure</u>, <u>that we may be clothed upon with robes of righteousness</u>, with palms in our hands, and <u>crowns of glory upon our heads</u>, and reap eternal joy for all our sufferings. O Lord God Almighty, hear us in these our petitions, and answer us from heaven, thy holy habitation, where thou sittest <u>enthroned, with glory, honor, power, majesty, might, dominion, truth, justice, judgment, mercy, and an infinity of fulness</u>, from everlasting to everlasting. <u>O hear, O hear, O hear us</u>, O Lord! And answer these petitions, and accept the dedication of this house unto thee, the work of our hands, which

we have built unto thy name... And help us by the power of thy Spirit, that we may mingle our voices with those bright, shining seraphs around thy throne, with acclamations of praise, singing Hosanna to God and the Lamb! And let these, <u>thine anointed ones, be clothed with salvation</u>, and thy saints shout aloud for joy. Amen, and Amen. (D&C 109:72-80)

I'm sure you noticed that the mighty string of nouns in the middle of that block are talking about God: He is enthroned "with glory, honor, power, majesty, might, dominion, [and] truth." But "he that receiveth my Father receiveth my Father's kingdom; therefore all that my Father hath shall be given unto him" (D&C 84:38). So although the prophet was speaking about God the Father, he was alluding to the blessing promised to *all* the faithful. (And this concept was taught in the Bible too in Revelation 21:7: "He that overcometh shall inherit all things; and I will be his God, and he shall be my son.")

In a later revelation, that idea was echoed more directly, and it was combined with this final, crowning ordinance we've been discussing:

> If a man marry a wife by my word, which is my law, and by the new and everlasting covenant, and it is <u>sealed</u> unto them <u>by the Holy Spirit</u> of promise, by him who is anointed, <u>unto whom I have appointed this power and the keys of this priesthood;</u> and it shall be said unto them—ye shall come forth in the first resurrection... and <u>shall inherit thrones, kingdoms, principalities, and powers, dominions, all heights and depths</u>... and if ye abide in my covenant... it shall be

done unto them in all things whatsoever my servant hath put upon them, <u>in time, and through all eternity</u>; and shall be of full force when they are out of the world; and they <u>shall pass by the angels</u>, and the gods, which are set there, <u>to their exaltation and glory</u> in all things, as hath been sealed upon their heads, which glory shall be a fulness and a continuation of the seeds forever and ever.

Then shall they be gods, because they have no end; therefore shall they be from everlasting to everlasting, because they continue; then shall they be above all, because all things are subject unto them. Then shall they be gods, because they have all power, and the angels are subject unto them. (D&C 132:19-20)

This doctrine of apotheosis, as you'll probably discover on your mission, makes some people angry—they see it as prideful, assuming, and cocky. First, Michael W. Fordham does an excellent job defending this perspective using only the Bible in an article called "Do We Have the Potential to become Like God?" It's definitely worth taking a look at. Second, I think we Mormons *do* have a tendency to become too prideful about it. The covenant is only effective when it's coupled with obedience, sacrifice, holiness, purity, and godliness—each of which are about *forgetting* the self and *not* seeking glory. Christ's gospel switches the paradigm so that he who would be greatest must be a servant. After all, our example God descended below all things—he became the lowest. Any saint who looks forward to commanding and controlling probably isn't worthy of such a position.

In summary, the sealing ordinance promises blessings

that are beyond what we can even imagine. But, again, it's a promise that's only fulfilled on the condition that the person remains faithful. That is, the Lord has the power to endow us with these unspeakable gifts, but only so long as we faithfully keep our part. Christ himself gave us a "promise immutable and unchangeable, that <u>inasmuch as those</u> whom I commanded <u>were faithful</u> they should be blessed with a multiplicity of blessings" (D&C 104:2).

44. The Sealing

When I was 22, I thought my body was invincible for the most part—at least for regular activities. And I'd only been home from my mission for about six months when it happened.

I was playing intramural basketball on a rubber with-con-crete-underneath floor. We were losing to a team that wasn't particularly good. I was frustrated about that, and, since those were my younger and meaner days, anger drove me to play my hardest. I lunged to block a simple pass, and when I landed, turning, I heard my knee pop, and I crumpled to the floor. Tev and our roommates helped me get home and then to a physician. I crutched on for a few days, till I got an MRI that showed a torn ACL and meniscus. After an arthroscopic surgery, it began to heal. But a few months later when I was playing basketball again, this time with the uncles at Thanksgiving, I tore that same ACL the rest of the way through. This led to a more serious surgery a few weeks later.

Poets have a Latin phrase they like to repeat: *memento mori*. It means, basically, "remember, we die." It implies that we ought to live life as fully as we can while it lasts—sort of another angle at *carpe diem*. Those months of crutching then limping across the Rexburg ice were one long *memento mori* for me. And I got pretty down. I'd always known, at least conceptually, the cold fact that my body was mortal and wouldn't last. But that was supposed to be a future thing, not a present thing.

When I finally saw the light on the other side (my knee's about 90% these days), I was a lot more grateful for it. I see my health now as a fleeting thing that I'm lucky to have. (And I do what I can to preserve and improve it—which ties in to holiness.) But the point of all this is that everything mortal will die. It's kind of a depressing truth. At least, if you don't know about the power that makes things Everlasting. It's called the sealing power. It brings bodies back to life, but it perpetuates virtues and relationships into immortality as well.

The temple ceremonies are conducted by God's authority—divine authority entrusted to mortals, which is a pattern that God established anciently. These priesthood keys, like those held by Peter of old, have the power to bind on earth and have those bindings continue in heaven.

> Elijah brought the keys of sealing powers—that power which seals a man to a woman and seals their posterity to them endlessly, that which seals their forefathers to them all the way back to Adam. This is the power and order that Elijah revealed—that same order of priesthood which God gave to Adam and to all the ancient patriarchs which followed after him. (Ezra

Taft Benson, "What I Hope You Will Teach Your Children about the Temple")

Because temple ordinances are officiated through this power, done by the Lord's authorized servants, they stand a chance at lasting through death. But it's not a show mortals can run entirely on their own—there's one other important piece: A member of the Godhead—the Holy Spirit—finalizes each immortalization. Temple covenants in particular are sealed—or made permanent—as the Spirit puts his stamp of approval on them, confirming that the participants have been faithful. The Lord explained it in section 132:

> All covenants, contracts, bonds, obligations, oaths, vows, performances, connections, associations, or expectations, that are not made and entered into and <u>sealed by the Holy Spirit</u> of promise, of him who is anointed, both as well <u>for time and for all eternity</u>, and that too most holy, by revelation and commandment <u>through the medium of mine anointed</u>, whom I have appointed on the earth to hold this power (and I have appointed unto my servant Joseph to hold this power in the last days, and there is never but one on the earth at a time on whom this power and the keys of this priesthood are conferred), are of no <u>efficacy, virtue, or force in and after the resurrection</u> from the dead; for all contracts that are not made unto this end have an end when men are dead. (D&C 132:7)

This warns that you shouldn't hope for a contract to be valid if you haven't met the divine requirements. But the converse is also true: If you *do* meet these requirements, the promises made in the covenants *will* be fulfilled. And, as we discussed, they're too great for us mortals to really wrap our minds around.

Just to clarify, the sealing *ceremony* is the union of a man and woman in matrimony—it's the final temple ordinance. The sealing *power* has a larger scope and wider reach—it's the power that must touch everything that becomes immortal. This sealing *power* is the center of the sealing *ceremony*:

> How did Adam bring his descendants into the presence of the Lord? The answer: <u>Adam and his descendants entered into the priesthood order of God</u>. Today we would say they went to the House of the Lord and received their blessings. The order of priesthood spoken of in the scriptures is sometimes referred to as <u>the patriarchal order</u> because it came down from father to son. But this order is otherwise described in modern revelation as an <u>order of family government</u> where a man and woman enter into a covenant with God—<u>just as did Adam and Eve</u>—<u>to be sealed for eternity, to have posterity, and to do the will and work of God</u> throughout their mortality. If a couple are true to their covenants, they are entitled to the blessing of the highest degree of the celestial kingdom. <u>These covenants today can only be entered into by going to the House of the Lord</u>. Adam followed this order and brought his posterity into the presence of God. He is the great example for us to follow. (Ezra Taft Benson,

"What I Hope You Will Teach Your Children about the Temple")

It's a big deal to make things immortal. And that's why the temple is so important. It makes both individuals and family bonds into metal so strong that they will outlast even time itself. Sooner or later, everything else is doomed to tear.

TEMPORAL MATTERS: SEALINGS

You're still a few years away from marriage, but that doesn't mean this talk about the sealing ceremony can't have significance to you now. It's a very important covenant, and the more you prepare, the better.

Also, once you receive your endowment, you can participate in proxy sealings. In other words, you'll be able to go through the entire ceremony before you've even met your eternal companion. It's not a bad idea to make a habit of doing sealings in your temple service so that you can prepare to personally make this capstone promise.

---

45. THE FAMILY

My buddy Seth has been a father for almost a year now. In light of that anniversary, I asked him what he'd learned, and this is what he said: When you get married, you kind of give up your *identity*—instead of being an *I*, you're a *we* (just like Elder Holland said about how *two* become *one*). With fatherhood, he went on to explain, you give up your *time*—it takes so much to raise a child that you basically have to give all you got (which hearkens back to consecration).

What he said really struck me. What a perfect way for the temple story to end—by sacrificing for your family as you promised in the covenants.

I've been lucky enough to attend several wedding ceremonies officiated by Grandpa Washburn—including those of our two married siblings. He always says that the couple is starting their own little kingdom—a king and queen destined to raise princes and princesses. That's the phrase he uses: "little kingdom." The sealing ordinance is what makes those little kingdoms possible.

> The divine plan of happiness enables family relationships to be perpetuated beyond the grave. Sacred ordinances and covenants available in holy temples make it possible for individuals to return to the presence of God and for families to be united eternally. (*The Family: A Proclamation to the World*)

In a divine marriage, one sealed for eternity, the husband and wife give themselves to each other—an act of humility, submission, and consecration. Together, and only together, they then enter the highest order of all, and they join God, righteously, in the act of creating and building his kingdom, both in mortality and throughout eternity:

> The gate to eternal life is celestial marriage, which holy order of matrimony enables the family unit to continue in eternity, so that the participating parties may have posterity as numerous as the sands upon the seashore or the stars in heaven. The Abrahamic

covenant enables men to create for themselves eternal family units that are patterned after the family of God our Heavenly Father. (*Pearl of Great Price Student Manual*)

This quote mentions the Abrahamic covenant, which we'll discuss more soon. First, let's talk about our more immediate ancestry: Grandpa Washburn. He's been quoted as saying, "We go to the temple to make covenants, but we go home to keep the covenants that we have made" (Elder Richard G. Scott even quoted this in his *Celebrating Celestial Marriage*). So even though the ceremony is over and that summative covenant has been made, it's not all finished. We have to hold fast—enduring to the end. Grandpa put it this way:

> The home is the testing ground. The home is the place where we learn to be more Christlike. The home is the place where we learn to overcome selfishness and give ourselves in service to others. I hope you will not think it simplistic [if I] suggest that it is the "little things" like <u>family prayer</u> and family <u>home evening</u> that are important: little things like a father helping his children say their <u>nightly prayers</u> and <u>telling them a bedtime story</u> instead of watching TV; little things like making time in the family schedule for <u>reading the scriptures</u>; little things like a husband being big enough to say, "Sweetheart, I'm sorry. I should not have said that. I'm going to do better," or a mother saying to a child, "I'm sorry I became angry. Please forgive me." Yes, it is the little things that we do each day and each week that make the difference. <u>By</u>

keeping the temple covenants, all of God's children
may be exalted. I say again that we go to the temple
to make the covenants, but we go home to keep those
covenants. (J Ballard Washburn, "The Temple Is a
Family Affair")

Pretty cool that he's our Grandpa. He's a great man.
But he became what he was because he was faithful in
these few small things. (In fact, I think his example of
a husband who needs to say sorry hits close to home—
he was never perfect, except in trying to be better.) In a
way, this home-centered perspective—the idea of a little
kingdom—makes the gospel seem very simple. But it is
really only an easy burden because husband and wife yoke
up with Lord, and his strength lifts them. As he promised
all who fight the good fight, "Inasmuch as ye are humble
and faithful and call upon my name, behold, I will give
you the victory" (D&C 104:82).

46. THE ABRAHAMIC COVENANT

As Mormon was compiling the records, he stopped his
narrative for a moment to poetically reflect on how the
Nephites had been so richly blessed (toward the end of
Helaman). This is one of my favorite passages of scripture,
partially because of its gallant imagery. He paints the
picture of a hero, sword in hand, crossing a treacherous
bridge over a pit of Dantean horrors:

Thus we may see that the Lord is merciful unto all
who will, in the sincerity of their hearts, call upon his

holy name. Yea, thus we see that <u>the gate of heaven is open</u> unto all, even to those who will believe on the name of Jesus Christ, who is the Son of God. Yea, we see that <u>whosoever will may lay hold upon the word of God</u>, which is quick and powerful, which <u>shall divide asunder</u> all the cunning and the snares and the wiles of the devil, and <u>lead the man of Christ</u> in a strait and narrow course across that everlasting gulf of misery which is prepared to engulf the wicked—and land their souls, yea, their immortal souls, <u>at the right hand of God in the kingdom of heaven</u>, to sit down with Abraham, and Isaac, and with Jacob, and with all our holy fathers, to go no more out. (Helaman 3:27-30)

And my favorite part, by far, is the last bit—that the end of the quest has "whosoever" (which in this case is the *everyman* wanderer) seated next to the heroic patriarchs—the ones it's easy to feel inferior to. He sits right next to them, the greatest of our human race, becoming ruler of many things by the grace of God. In other words, even a simple guy like me or a young kid like you have this offered to us. It's pretty incredible. What's more, he writes, "at the right hand of God," which again echoes this idea that we're "heirs of God and joint-heirs with Christ."

The Lord also made this promise to modern saints directly:

> I will bear [the faithful servant] up as on eagles' wings; and he shall beget glory and honor to himself and unto my name, that when he shall finish his work I may receive him unto myself, even as I did my servant David Patten, who is with me at this time, and also my

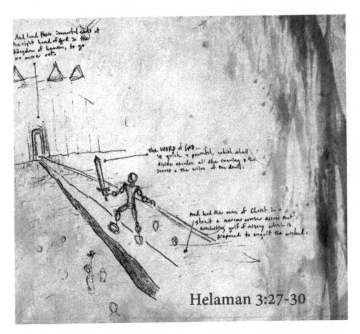

And lead their immortal souls at the right hand of God in the Kingdom of heaven, to go no more out.

the WORD of God... is quick & powerful, which shall divide asunder all the cunning & the snares & the wiles of the devil.

And lead the men of Christ in a strait & narrow course across that everlasting gulf of misery which is prepared to engulf the wicked.

Helaman 3:27-30

servant Edward Partridge, and also my aged servant Joseph Smith, Sen., who sitteth with Abraham at his right hand, and blessed and holy is he, for he is mine. (D&C 124:18-19)

Let's look deeper into what it means to be heirs alongside Abraham and his sons. God himself said to Abraham, "I will multiply your seed as the stars of heaven, and all this land that I have spoken of will I give unto your seed, and they shall inherit it for ever" (Ex. 32:13). God made him great promises, which were, for the most part, the same promises he'd made with Adam and to all the faithful prophets. Those same promises are extended to Abraham's posterity, including those who aren't direct descendants but who are spiritually adopted in.

Elder McConkie gave an excellent summary of the Abrahamic covenant which can be found in the Bible Dictionary (and I've added numbers to distinguish the parts):

> Abraham first received the gospel by baptism (which is the [1] covenant of salvation). Then he had conferred upon him the higher priesthood, and he entered into celestial marriage (which is the [2] covenant of exaltation), gaining [3] assurance thereby that he would have eternal increase. Finally he received a promise that [4] all of these blessings would be offered to all of his mortal posterity. Included in the divine promises to Abraham were the assurances that [5] Christ would come through his lineage, and that [6] Abraham's posterity would receive certain lands as an eternal inheritance. These promises taken together are called the Abrahamic covenant. It was renewed with Isaac and again with Jacob. The portions of the covenant that pertain to personal salvation and eternal increase [1, 2, 3] are renewed with each individual who receives the ordinance of celestial marriage. Those of non-Israelite lineage, commonly known as gentiles, are adopted into the house of Israel, and become heirs of the covenant and the seed of Abraham, through the ordinances of the gospel.

God's grace offers exaltation to everyone, in spite of status, bloodline, or birthright. I find a lot of hope in that fact—that even his very greatest promises are offered to regular people. And we can access this grace by becoming worthy to enter the temple and then by remembering the promises we make there.

47. PERSONAL STUDY

Scriptures

- D&C 109 (the prayer offered at the dedication of Kirtland Temple in 1836, which, according to the Prophet, was given to him by revelation)
- D&C 132 (the revelation relating to the new and everlasting covenant, including the eternity of the marriage covenant)
- "The Family: A Proclamation to the World" (the official declaration)

Sermons

- "What I Hope You Will Teach Your Children about the Temple" by Ezra Taft Benson
- "A House of Glory" by Hugh Nibley

Go to jwashburn.com/books/dearjeff for links to these readings and a complete bibliography.

AFTERTHOUGHTS

I will fill this house with glory... In this place will I give peace.

— *Haggai 2:7, 9*

We've covered the whole temple experience, including the three main parts: initiatory, endowment, and sealing.

This next section may seem a little sporadic. It is.

It's a series of vignettes that didn't fit well into previous sections. They all relate to the temple in one way or another. Some will immediately strike you as important. Others may make more sense after you've studied a bit more and have attended the temple a few times.

48. WHERE ART THOU?

I have a goal to be a transparent communicator.

This may come from my being an essayist—I need to be brutally honest about everything my keyboard touches, my own soul most of all. And being honest on paper has bled into my social life. I've dared my friends to "ask me anything you want." And I like to think that I'm ready (even if hesitant) to be forthright about whatever they might ask. (Don't get me wrong—I'm nowhere near to upholding this ideal perfectly—but I strive for it.)

I believe that if you can't own up to what you're doing, you probably shouldn't be doing it. In other words, if you're embarrassed about something, you have two options: Stop being embarrassed, or stop doing the thing. For example, if you're watching *Avatar: The Last Airbender*, you either need to own up to the fact that you're watching a kid's show, or you need to quit watching it. But you shouldn't sneak it—that's the bottom line. (Now's a fair time to admit that I occasionally throw fire-bender punches into the air when no one's looking.)

Right after Adam and Eve partook of the fruit of the tree

of knowledge, the Lord came back to the garden and "called unto Adam [asking]... Where art thou?" (Genesis 3:9). They had just passed from their state of innocence: They knew good and evil, and, right then, they were embarrassed about God catching them off guard like that—embarrassed enough that they hid.

"Where art thou?" is an important question—one we should be ready to answer at any time. Hopefully that motivates us toward goodness.

The psalmist took this commission to heart—the words of a wanderer ready to answer without reservation: "Search me, O God, and know my heart: try me, and know my thoughts: and see if there be any wicked way in me, and lead me in the way everlasting" (Psalms 139:23-24).

49. KAPH

I once heard a member of the Provo Temple Presidency teach our stake conference about the semitic letter *kaph*. *Kaph* looks like this: ﻙ. It's the 11th letter of most semitic alphabets (e.g., Arabic, Hebrew, and Persian), and it originates from a pictogram of a hand (as Wikipedia says, "in both modern Arabic and modern Hebrew, *kaph* means palm"). He said that it—a cupping hand turned upward—represents a soul who is prepared to receive the blessings from above that God has prepared for the worthy.

50. EZEKIEL'S TEMPLE VISION

Here's a story from *The Old Testament* a lot of people aren't familiar with (I noticed it thanks to S. Michael

Wilcox's "House of Glory"). It's from a vision given to Ezekiel, a revelation that spans many chapters. Ezekiel wrote that "in the visions of God" he was taken "upon a very high mountain" where he met a man "whose appearance was like... brass." As the two of them began to talk, the angel asked him questions and led him from place to place, instructing him as they went. The angel explained that Ezekiel was brought there "for to the intent that I might show [these things] unto thee," so he could then explain it to the rest of Israel. He continues his narration:

> [The angel] brought me again unto the door of [the temple]; and, behold, <u>waters issued out from under the threshold of the house eastward</u>... [Then he] led me about the way without unto the utter gate... that looketh eastward; and, behold, there ran out waters on the right side. And when the man that had the line in his hand [the angel] went forth eastward, he measured a thousand cubits, and he brought me through the waters; the waters were <u>to the ankles</u>. [Thrice more] he measured a thousand... [and] the waters were <u>to the knees</u>... [and then] <u>to the loins</u>. [And afterward] it was a river that I could not pass over: for the waters were risen, <u>waters to swim in</u>... And he said unto me, "Son of man, hast thou seen this?" Then he brought me... to the brink of the river. [And] behold, at the bank of the river were very many trees on the one side and on the other. Then said he unto me, "These waters issue out toward the east country, and go down into the desert, and go into the sea: which being brought forth into the sea, the waters shall be healed. And

it shall come to pass, that <u>every thing that liveth,</u> <u>which moveth, whithersoever the rivers shall come,</u> <u>shall live</u>... <u>for they shall be healed</u>... And by the river upon the bank... shall grow all trees for meat, whose leaf shall not fade, neither shall the fruit thereof be consumed: It shall bring forth new fruit according to his months, <u>because their waters they issued out of</u> <u>the sanctuary</u>: and the fruit thereof shall be for meat, and the leaf thereof for medicine." (Ezekiel 47:1-12)

This story has three features I'd like to point out:

First, this dream has been symbolically reflected in the architecture of many temples—they build fountains near the eastward-facing front doors as a reminder of Ezekiel's vision and the things it promised.

Second, the imagery from his vision is symbolic—how the water gets deeper and deeper. It parallels the way the Lord helps us to learn line upon line and precept upon precept—slow, but steady. We ought to be eager not only to get our feet wet, but to keep going until we are fully swimming in the waters of life.

And, finally, the water—the substance which flows from the temple—gives life to everything it touches—both healing and sustenance.

51. Jacob's Ladder

The Story

Esau was angry at Jacob for taking his birthright and then his blessing—angry enough to kill. So Jacob, hearkening his mother's advice to flee, set out across the desert from Beer-sheba to his uncle's in Haran, far to the north. On that journey, he had to camp out in the middle of nowhere, and he even used stones for his pillow. That night he had a dream—perhaps a vision.

He saw a ladder or stairway that began on earth and stretched all the way up to heaven (touching earth *and* heaven is significant). Next he saw the Lord standing in the space above the stairway, and the Lord spoke, promising to grant Jacob the same blessings given to Abraham—he made Jacob a joint heir. He also promised Jacob that "in thee and in thy seed shall all the families of the earth be blessed" (Genesis 28:14), which is a promise we, as Ephraimites, get to live up to. And then, since Jacob was wandering away from his home into a strange land, the Lord comforted him, saying, "I am with thee, and will keep thee in all places whither thou goest, and will bring thee again into this land; for I will not leave thee" (Genesis 28:15). So the Lord promised to stay with him during his pilgrimage.

When the dream ended, Jacob knew he'd seen "the gate of heaven"—the gate of heaven! What an awesome way to phrase it. And he was so impressed by this vision that he got up and built a monument of stones—using the same rocks he'd slept on. Then he consecrated the monument with oil and dedicated it: "This stone, which I have set for a pillar, shall be God's house." In other words, he had built God's house—a temple—so that he could remember the things God had taught and promised him. And he re-named the site *Beth-El*, which means "house of *El*" or "house of the Lord." And he made a promise that God would "be my God"—professing his intention to make sacrifices to the God who'd promised him so much (Genesis 28).

The Scope

President Marion G. Romney said, "Jacob realized that the covenants he made with the Lord there were the rungs on the ladder that he himself would have to climb in order to obtain the promised blessings—blessings that would entitle him to enter heaven and associate with the Lord" (*Old Testament Student Manual* 86)—the mortal path leading to the eternal heavens. And I love that phrase "entitle him to enter heaven."

In *The Divine Comedy*, Dante, walking through the afterlife, sees this same ladder—Jacob's ladder—and as he peers upward, it's so high he can't see the top! This is brilliant—it reminds me how little we know about the divinity that stretches above us. We mortals can see the part that is just within our grasp, but we can't imagine just how high it goes (going back to 1 Corinthians 2:9, "Eye hath not seen, nor ear heard, neither have entered into the heart of man, the things which God hath prepared for them that love him"). Joseph Smith added,

> When you climb up a ladder, you must begin at the bottom, and ascend step by step, until you arrive at the top; and so it is with the principles of the Gospel—you must begin with the first, and go on until you learn all the principles of exaltation. But it will be a great while after you have passed through the veil before you will have learned them. It is not all to be comprehended in this world; it will be a great work to learn our salvation and exaltation even beyond the grave. (*Teachings of the Prophet Joseph Smith* 348)

The Symbol

A certain motif appears in the architecture of many modern temples, the Timpanogos Temple in particular. The symbol is two vertical lines leading upward to a circle of infinity—which Tev explained to me is a stylized representation of Jacob's Ladder. Here's how I make sense of that: A circle can represent the eternities of heaven, and the posts extending up to it are like a pathway (or ladder)—a pathway leading from earth below to eternity above.

The Song

One of my favorite hymns—"Nearer, My God, to Thee" (#100, whose lyrics were written by Sarah F. Adams)—retells the story of Jacob's ladder. The temple teaches us how to get nearer to our God. I love this. It illuminates the pathway that leads to him:

1.
Nearer, my God, to thee, Nearer to thee!
E'en though it be a cross That raiseth me.
Still all my song shall be Nearer, my God, to thee,
Nearer, my God, to thee, Nearer to thee!

2.
Though like the wanderer, The sun gone down,
Darkness be over me, My rest a stone,
Yet in my dreams I'd be Nearer, my God, to thee,
Nearer, my God, to thee, Nearer to thee!

3.
There let the way appear, Steps unto heav'n;
All that thou sendest me, In mercy giv'n;
Angels to beckon me Nearer, my God, to thee,
Nearer, my God, to thee, Nearer to thee!
4.
Then with my waking thoughts Bright with thy praise,
Out of my stony griefs Bethel I'll raise;
So by my woes to be Nearer, my God, to thee,
Nearer, my God, to thee, Nearer to thee!

5.
Or if, on joyful wing Cleaving the sky,
Sun, moon, and stars forgot, Upward I fly,
Still all my song shall be Nearer, my God, to thee,
Nearer, my God, to thee, Nearer to thee!

52. THE OPPOSITE OF PRIESTHOOD

Sometimes the gospel can seem a little gender lopsided. Much of the scriptures talk about men without telling the stories of women. The patriarchal order is organized by tracing a line through fatherhood. (As an interesting side note, the Navajos of Arizona, where I served my mission, traditionally traced lineage through a matriarchal line.) Along those lines, I'd like to walk you through a thought experiment—a series of questions—that may help in some of your future temple conversations.

First, what is the opposite of *motherhood*?

It's *fatherhood*, isn't it?

But in the church it's sometimes said that men get to hold the priesthood while women get a complimentary gift, which is motherhood. If we turn it into a diagram, it would look like this:

MALE	FEMALE
~~Priesthood~~	Motherhood

It's actually a nice way to think of it. But those two aren't really opposites, are they? As we said, *fatherhood* is the opposite of *motherhood*. So we need to rearrange the diagram:

MALE	FEMALE
Fatherhood	Motherhood
Priesthood	?

Next question: What is the opposite of priesthood?

It's not so easy to answer (if the opposite isn't *motherhood*, which it isn't). But I promise there's an answer. Instead, why not think of it this way: What is the opposite of *priest*?

A nun, I think I hear you saying. And you're on the right track.

What is the opposite of *actor?* You said *actress*, right?

What's the opposite of *seamster? Seamstress.*

What's the opposite of *prince? Princess.*

Before the female forms started dropping out of our English language, this used to work with *mister* and *mistress*, *governor* and *governess*, *painter* and *paintress*, and I wish so bad that we could say *photographer* and *photographress*. But you get the point.

BE STRONG
AND OF GOOD COURAGE.
YOU ARE TRULY
RYAL
S P I R I T
DAUGHTERS
OF ALMIGHTY GOD.
❧ YOU ARE
PRINCESSES
DESTINED TO BECOME QUEENS.

YOUR OWN WONDROUS
STORY HAS ALREADY BEGUN.

YOUR
Once
Upon a
Time
IS NOW.

— PRESIDENT DIETER F. UCHTDORF

The opposite of a priest, then, is a priestess.

And we can complete our diagram above with a word that sounds a little unusual but that makes logical sense: *Priestesshood.*

And I'll leave it at that.

53. CIRCUMSCRIBE

In this book, I've drawn on Buddhism a little. And I've alluded to Star Wars and Indiana Jones. I didn't mention it in here, but I really enjoy Stephen Hawking's books too, and he's an agnostic. But pulling from these sources is okay, and I'll tell you why. As Mormons, our beliefs are very simple:

We believe in everything that's true.

That's it. That's our religion in a nutshell—discovering and embracing truth, no matter what divine or earthly source it may come from. As Mormon preached to his crumbling people,

> The Spirit of Christ is given to every man, that he may know good from evil; wherefore, I show unto you the way to judge; for every thing which inviteth to do good, and to persuade to believe in Christ, is sent forth by the power and gift of Christ; wherefore ye may know with a perfect knowledge it is of God. (Moroni 7:16)

In other words, if you find something that invites you toward good, you can rest assured it's something Godly. Joseph Smith put it like this:

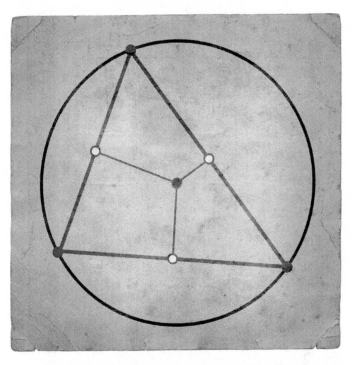

One of the grand fundamental principles of Mormonism is to receive truth, let it come from where it may. (Nauvoo Temple sermon, 9 July 1843)

The doctrine of the Latter-day Saints is truth... The first and fundamental principle of our holy religion is that we believe that we have a right to embrace all, and every item of truth, without limitation or without being circumscribed or prohibited by the creeds or superstitious notions of men, or by the dominations of one another, when that truth is clearly demonstrated to our minds, and we have the highest degree of evidence of the same. (Letter from Joseph Smith in Liberty Jail to Isaac Galland, 22 March 1839)

Not only is that a tenant of our earthly religion, Joseph taught that it will continue to go in that direction in eternity:

> He who scattered Israel has promised to gather them; therefore inasmuch as you are to be instrumental in this great work, he will endow you with power, wisdom, might, and intelligence, and every qualification necessary; while your minds will expand wider and wider, until you can circumscribe the earth and the heavens, reach forth into eternity, and contemplate the mighty acts of Jehovah in all their variety and glory. (Joseph Smith, *History of the Church* 4:129)

This is why God himself recommended we search for and read the "best books" (D&C 88:118, 109:7). It's this idea of eagerly gathering up truth into our arms, and holding our hands out to receive more. In fact, in both of these quotes Joseph Smith used an interesting word that implies this same imagery:

Circumscribe \ˈsər-kəm-ˌskrīb\ transitive verb
- To draw a line or circle around something
- To surround with a boundary
- To construct a geometrical figure so as to touch as many points as possible

54. Family History

People always say family history work is hard, but it doesn't have to be. I'll teach you how to hack the process—how to do family names in two simple steps:

1. Call Uncle Rich and ask him to send you some names.

2. Take the PDF he emails you to the desk where they print the blue cards.

It's a cinch. I don't know why people always complain about how hard it is.

Seriously though, doing work for people who never got the chance is important. It's a Christlike service—particularly because it's something they can't do for themselves. It's also great that doing this work means we get to return to the temple often (if we only went once, it would be much harder to learn from the temple ceremony).

I'm not going to dive into family-history research here. Partially because I'm inexperienced and partially because that's not the point of this book. This book is to help you prepare for *your* first time—to maximize your single, personal experience. After you've gone once, you'll be a veteran, and you'll have the future to study the temple *and* family history as much as you want. And you'll be ready to mount a rescue mission for your ancestors.

But to keep you excited to do work for the dead, I'd like to share a story from Joseph F. Smith. He wondered how Christ, in the short time that his body was in the tomb, could have preached to all the spirits in their spiritual prison:

> And as I wondered, my eyes were opened, and my understanding quickened, and I perceived that the Lord went not in person among the wicked and the disobedient who had rejected the truth, to teach them; but behold, from among the righteous, <u>he organized his forces</u> and appointed messengers, <u>clothed with power and authority</u>, and commissioned them <u>to</u>

go forth and carry the light of the gospel to them that were in darkness, even to all the spirits of men; and thus was the gospel preached to the dead. And the chosen messengers went forth to declare the acceptable day of the Lord and proclaim liberty to the captives who were bound, even unto all who would repent of their sins and receive the gospel. (D&C 138:29-31)

Many spirits, including our own ancestors, never had the assurance and peace the gospel brings. And so they're sitting, like that quote says, in spiritual darkness. We have the duty to help Christ in bringing that light to them, and a big part is doing the physical ordinances on their behalf.

55. THE ESSENCE

In a vision, John saw the kingdom of heaven descending onto earth. And he observed, strangely, that it had no temples, which he then explained:

[I saw a city] having the glory of God... The street of the city was pure gold, as it were transparent glass. And I saw no temple therein: for the Lord God Almighty and the Lamb are the temple of it. (Revelation 21:11, 21-22)

The temple is a holy place where only worthy elements and souls are allowed. It's also a place to come into the presence of God. If the entire earth is purged of unworthy elements, and if God and his Son dwell there, then the earth itself will be a temple.

56. Pay the Price

President Booth taught us another valuable life lesson: "Pay the price." Part of what he meant by that is embodied by the 10,000-hour rule—10,000 hours, they say, is how long it takes to become an expert in any given field (Malcolm Gladwell in *Outliers* argues this was true of both The Beatles and Bill Gates). President Booth expected us to set high goals and then work hard to achieve them—on the mission and afterwards—in all areas, from financial investing to spiritual matters. There are great things to be had in this life and the next, but they'll be gained only by those who are willing to pay the price.

Now what does this have to do with the temple?

The Lord taught in *The Doctrine and Covenants* that because "I will own them, and they shall be mine in that day when I shall come to make up my jewels... they must needs be chastened and tried, even as Abraham, who was commanded to offer up his only son" (D&C 101:3-4). Abraham was asked to give up the thing that was most precious to him. But he proved he was willing. He trusted the Lord, and he did it. And now he lives with that legacy.

Hugh Nibley weighed in on this in a lecture called *Faith of an Observer*:

> *We* must do the works of Abraham. We are told specifically in *The Doctrine and Covenants* that means sacrificing, if necessary, your own life. Abraham was willing to do that, and everyone at some time or another will have the opportunity to show that [same willingness]. Remember... Abraham was tested to the last extreme... Unless you are willing to give

everything, you cannot claim eternal life. It's not to be cheaply bought. These are the great blessings of Abraham, Isaac, and Jacob... they must be willing even to give life itself, and so forth... This Abraham, who towers like a colossus, is *everyman*, as every man should be... Remember what the Lord promised the Apostles: "In this world ye shall have tribulation. But be of good cheer. I have overcome the world."

This reflects back on our discussion about giving up this world's treasures for those of a better—being "willing to march into hell for a heavenly cause" ("Man of La Mancha"). Sometimes it may seem like a harsh doctrine. But how can we expect to sit next to Abraham and the patriarchs if we're not willing to submit as fully as they did?

By sacrificing—by letting go—it changes who we are. It makes us into people whose hands aren't full of mortal things—so we're ready to receive heavenly things. Which reminds me again of C. S. Lewis's logic: "You must have a capacity to receive, or even omnipotence can't give" (*A Grief Observed*). By making these tough choices and giving up the things we cling to, we make ourselves ready to receive omnipotent gifts.

57. THE CONGREGATION

In the chapter on the initiatory, we looked at Exodus 40:12-13, which says to "bring Aaron and his sons unto the door of the tabernacle of the congregation," where they would be washed, anointed, clothed, and sanctified. But I want you to notice one specific phrase: "the tabernacle of the congregation."

In our modern usage, the word *congregation* usually means a large group of people. But the ancient Israelite tabernacle was a portable tent, and it wasn't very big—only about 15-feet wide and three times that long. It couldn't have fit a "congregation," and it wasn't meant to. That's because the tabernacle had a different purpose.

A *congregation*, in this case, meant "the meeting of two people" (i.e., "we met," or "we congregated"). The tabernacle was a place where a congregation was supposed to happen—where two people were supposed to meet.

These two people were the high priest and the Lord.

Elder James E. Talmage puts it like this:

> [The Hebrew refers to the tabernacle as] *Ohel Moed*, the best authenticated translation of which is the "Tent of Meeting." Let it not be supposed, however, that this means in the ordinary sense a meeting-house... but <u>the place of communion between God and His Priesthood</u>. The Tent of Meeting, or the Tabernacle of the Congregation, in Israel, was the Lord's tent wherein He met the authorized representatives of His people... (*The House of the Lord* 26)

> The all-pervading and all-controlling thought in the erection of this portable sanctuary was that of expressing <u>the close association between Jehovah and His people</u>. The people were to consider themselves specifically the people of God, and amongst them should be His dwelling, surpassing in a transcendent degree the presence of the gods of wood and stone

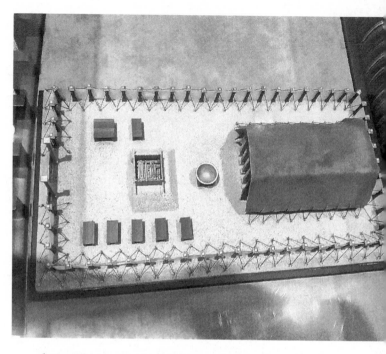

housed among the idolatrous nations with whom Israel had to contend. This thought was expressed in the earliest commandment respecting the building of the Tabernacle: "<u>And let them make me a sanctuary that I may dwell among them</u>" (Exodus 25:8)... (27) Critical scholars specify the following features characteristic of the Temple of Solomon and lacking in the Temple of Zerubbabel: (1) <u>the Ark</u> of the Covenant; (2) <u>the sacred fire</u>; (3) the Shekinah, or glory of the Lord, manifested of old as <u>the Divine Presence</u>; (4) <u>the Urim and Thummim</u>, by which Jehovah made plain His will to the priests of the Aaronic order; (5) the genius or <u>spirit of prophecy</u>, indicative of the closest communion between mortals and their God. (51)

By the same token, our modern temples could be called temples of the congregation.

58. SHECHINAH

"The Lord is in his holy temple: let all the earth keep silence before him" (Habakkuk 2:20).

It's easy to think of that as a figurative thing. In fact, I often find it difficult to convert the stories I read in the scriptures into something more literal—something I believe could actually happen in my own contemporary world. But the doctrine is clear—the mortal boundaries of this world are not impenetrable. Both symbolic and literal miracles can and do happen. And that means, too, that the Lord really does stand in his own temple, even today.

There's an interesting entry in the Bible Dictionary under *shechinah* (הניכש). It's another Hebrew word (we've learned quite a few), and it means "the dwelling" or, perhaps better, "the presence."

> [It's] a word used by the later Jews (and borrowed from them by the Christians) to denote the cloud of brightness and glory that marked the presence of the Lord, as spoken of in Exodus 3:1-6 and 24:16, 1 Kings 8:10, Isaiah 6:1-3, Matthew 17:5, and Acts 7:55. The Prophet Joseph Smith described this phenomenon in connection with his first vision, as a "light... above the brightness of the sun," and said that he saw two Personages whose "brightness and glory defy all description," standing "in the light."

We've already discussed how Nephi, like his prophet hero Isaiah, saw the Lord, as did his little brother and his father. "The Lord [also] spake unto Moses face to face, as a man speaketh unto his friend..." which gave Moses the courage to make a request, as they spoke: "Now therefore, I pray thee, if I have found grace in thy sight, show me now thy way, that I may know thee..." (Exodus 33:11,13). This happened to Enoch too, which he wrote in his temple journal:

> As I was journeying, and stood upon the place Mahujah, and cried unto the Lord, there came a voice out of heaven, saying, "Turn ye, and get ye upon the mount Simeon." And it came to pass that I turned and went up on the mount; and... I beheld the heavens open, and I was clothed upon with glory; and I saw the Lord; and he stood before my face, and he talked with me, even as a man talketh one with another, face to face; and he said unto me, "Look, and I will show unto thee the world for the space of many generations." (Moses 7:2-4)

So, along with witnessing the *shechinah*, Enoch saw the history of the world through some divine method—a mortal was given the mental wherewithal to consume a godly portion of knowledge. (Of course, he wasn't the only one to get this sort of tour.)

As the Lord was teaching the latter-day church about priesthood—how it was passed from father to son, through Adam, Enoch, Noah, Melchizedek, and Abraham—he taught that it holds a key related to the *shechinah*:

And this greater priesthood [the one named after Melchizedek] administereth the gospel and holdeth the key of the mysteries of the kingdom, even the key of the knowledge of God. Therefore, in the ordinances thereof, the power of godliness is manifest. And without the ordinances thereof, and the authority of the priesthood, the power of godliness is not manifest unto men in the flesh; for without this no man can see the face of God, even the Father, and live. Now this Moses plainly taught to the children of Israel in the wilderness, and sought diligently to sanctify his people that they might behold the face of God. (D&C 84:19-23)

I haven't emphasized priesthood authority much in this book, but it's important, largely because it holds the key to this great privilege—the mysteries. Without it, none of us can walk the path we've been discussing—the one that brings us back to our home, to be in the presence of our Father. And I love that "Moses plainly taught [this] to the children of Israel." It's been taught to us plainly enough too—to those who hearken.

Oliver Cowdery, who was president of the Quorum of the Twelve, gave this charge to his fellow Apostles: "Never cease striving until you have seen God face to face... *Jacob*, you know, wrestled till *he* had obtained" (*History of the Church* 2:195). He *wrestled* with a divine being right before he got his new name—a real struggle, not some casual approach to God and godhood. To pull out some key words from Moses's story, he *diligently sought sanctification*. That's what

President Cowdery was asking of his troops—he wanted them to strive.

It's easy to justify putting his pep talk aside—after all, President Cowdery was speaking to Apostles, not common men like you and me. But if we think that, we'll make that our future—a self-fulfilling prophecy. If we *don't* strive, we'll never get to where we might have gotten if we had.

In other words, whether we reach it or not, we'll be better for having tried.

I don't know if I'll ever be made of the mettle, while I'm a mortal, to receive this highest of privileges. But I'm trying my hardest to keep *hoping* for such a thing. Just like Nephi and Jacob did.

The psalmist wrote it this way—a beautiful metaphor, because we can't go long without drinking *water* either:

> My soul thirsteth for God, for the living God: when shall I come and appear before [him]? (Psalms 42:2)

59. JESUS APPEARS

The ancients saw Christ.

But their writing process, and whatever transcription and translation that happened afterward, seemed to limit what we now have to read. Fortunately, a modern prophet shared it with us more plainly. I have nothing to say that's more profound than the passage itself, so here are Joseph's words for you to read and think about:

> The veil was taken from our minds, and the eyes of our understanding were opened. We saw the Lord standing upon the breastwork of the pulpit, before

us; and under his feet was a paved work of pure gold, in color like amber. His eyes were as a flame of fire; the hair of his head was white like the pure snow; his countenance shone above the brightness of the sun; and his voice was as the sound of the rushing of great waters, even the voice of Jehovah, saying:

I am the first and the last; I am he who liveth, I am he who was slain; I am your advocate with the Father. Behold, your sins are forgiven you; you are clean before me; therefore, lift up your heads and rejoice. Let the hearts of your brethren rejoice, and let the hearts of all my people rejoice, who have, with their might, built this house to my name. For behold, I have accepted this house, and my name shall be here; and I will manifest myself to my people in mercy in this house. Yea, I will appear unto my servants, and speak unto them with mine own voice, if my people will keep my commandments, and do not pollute this holy house. Yea the hearts of thousands and tens of thousands shall greatly rejoice in consequence of the blessings which shall be poured out, and the endowment with which my servants have been endowed in this house. And the fame of this house shall spread to foreign lands; and this is the beginning of the blessing which shall be poured out upon the heads of my people. Even so. Amen. (D&C 110:1-10)

60. STRONGER THAN SIGHT

When Grandpa Washburn was president of the Las Vegas Temple, he was asked on more than one occasion, inappropriately, I think, whether he had seen Jesus in the temple. (It's inappropriate because if he were to answer *yes* he might be desecrating a sacred experience.) Grandpa would always answer like this: "No, I haven't seen Jesus in the temple. But I've had the privilege"—and he'd fight back the emotions right here—"I've had the privilege of spending every day in this temple with a member of the Godhead." And what he meant by that was that he'd been blessed to have the Holy Ghost with him.

President Harold B. Lee spoke about this Spirit, which can give you knowledge that's stronger than eyesight:

> The most powerful witness you can have that [the Savior] lives comes when the power of the Holy Spirit bears witness to your soul that He *does* live. More powerful than sight, more powerful than walking and talking with Him, is that witness of the Spirit... The Lord said in a revelation to the early leaders, "I will tell you in your mind and in your heart by the Holy Ghost. It shall dwell within you. This is the revelation by which Moses led the children of Israel to the Red Sea and on across it." When that Spirit has witnessed to our spirit, that's a revelation from Almighty God. (*Teachings of Presidents of the Church: Harold B. Lee*)

We mortals tend to put a lot of stock in our capacity to physically see things—whether we can get close enough to catch some of the photons that bounce off an object. But there are definitely more important types of knowledge. For example, there's no way to directly see our Mom's love (although you can see the fruits of her love). But just because it can't be seen doesn't mean it isn't real.

But that's an abstract thing, and we're talking about seeing the physical presence of a physical God—a God who walked in sandals and ate fish and honeycomb. There will be a time when we know him like that, and it's coming. For now, though, the conviction we have in our hearts—a feeling made firm by the Spirit—is a more valuable thing than actually seeing.

Let's go back to our archetype: Imagine you're in the wilderness, far from home. You have the abstract memory in your mind and perhaps a hope in your heart that your home's still there, miles away. And yet your eyes can't currently prove to you that it exists. You, the wanderer in this situation, have to trust your mind and heart, not your eyes, enough to start walking in the right direction. And it's only in walking in that direction that your eyes will finally confirm what your heart told you long ago.

Your pilgrim vision—your imagination, your hope, and the Spirit that's inside you—can create a stronger drive than seeing the actual place. Some others, squatters, you might say, who are unwilling to start the journey, may see the place with their own eyes afar off. But they're indifferent. Seeing creates no stirring in their hearts, and they take the thing for granted. But to you the wanderer, the whisperings from inside—stronger than sight—will inspire you to journey.

61. ADIEU

And <u>an highway</u> shall be there... and it <u>shall be called</u>
<u>the way of holiness</u>; <u>the unclean shall not pass over it</u>;
but it shall be for those: the wayfaring men, though
fools, shall not err therein. No lion shall be there,
nor any ravenous beast shall go up thereon... but <u>the</u>
<u>redeemed shall walk there</u>: and the ransomed of the
Lord shall return, and come to Zion with songs and
everlasting joy upon their heads: they shall obtain
joy and gladness, and <u>sorrow and sighing shall flee</u>
<u>away</u>. (Isaiah 35:8-9)

A road called the way of holiness—it's another majestic
image. That's the road we want.

I know that Christ will guide his wandering soldiers
home. I really do believe in this road—that apotheosis
is actually possible. There's happiness out there that's far
greater than the best things we've experienced or can even
imagine.

I love you. Thanks for being an awesome brother and a
good example to me.

I'll close with words that Paul wrote to his friend and
brother Timothy:

Meditate upon these things; give thyself wholly to
them; that thy profiting may appear to all. (1 Timothy
4:15)

—J

62. PERSONAL STUDY

Scripture

- Genesis 28:10-22 (the story of Jacob's Ladder)

Sermons

- "The Two Trees" by Valerie Hudson Cassler
- "The Meaning of the Temple" by Hugh Nibley

Go to jwashburn.com/books/dearjeff for links to these readings and a complete bibliography.

Thy servant has sought thee earnestly;
now I have found thee.

— *Abraham 2:12*

FEEL FREE
TO EMAIL ME TOO!
ME@JWASHBURN.COM

Thanks for Reading

As you probably know, I'm a self-published indie author. That means this is an artisan book, hand-crafted from beginning to end. I appreciate your support. I'm glad that you read, and I hope you enjoyed it.

If you have a couple minutes, I'd love to have you post a review on Amazon. I read every one, and getting your feedback is great. It also helps other readers discover my books. It will help me more than you may realize. (Even a sentence will do.)

Also, I have a few other books I bet you'll enjoy. (And if you don't enjoy them, Amazon has a generous 7-day return policy, so there's no risk to you.) Other readers have been loving them and posting excellent reviews. I think you should check out *Ecksdot* in particular—it's the sort of adventure that will make you wish you were a kid again.

If you want to know when I release more books in the future, sign up for my monthly letter at www.jwashburn.com. (I occasionally give away free books and merchandise to subscribers too.)

And finally, I'd like to keep in touch with you. I'm on Goodreads, Google+, Facebook, and Twitter. And make sure you say hi if we're ever at an event together.

Well, thanks again. And I mean it.

I couldn't do what I do without you.

— J

A Brief Excerpt from ECKSDOT

A Wise Brother

I was lying on my back, on the top bunk, talking to the ceiling. Zach was lying below me.

"You know that dream I had last night?"

"Yeah?"

"I dreamed I had to get this little metal thingie with a red cross on it. And it was inside a white barn. Well, today on the way home I realized it was the barn at the end of our street—the exact same one."

"Hmm. Weird."

"Yeah, way weird. So we decided to try to get in."

The bed shook as he shifted. "You did?"

"Yeah, but no luck. It's all locked up."

"Don't you think you might get in trouble? Get caught or something?"

"Yeah, we almost got caught already. But my dream was telling me to go inside."

"Nate, maybe you forgot, but it wasn't a dream, it was a nightmare."

"Yeah, but..."

"You're going to follow a nightmare?"

"It wasn't the nightmare part that was telling me that. The nightmare came after."

"Oh, sure, so *after* you sneak into someone else's locked-up barn, the nightmare happens."

J WASHBURN

ECKSDOT

Dreams bleed out from all minds.

What Readers Are Saying about ECKSDOT

"A very original world with an ingenious set of rules."
— KMK

"I was blown away with how Washburn nailed the mind of a sixth-grader. It was simply fantastic. Reading this book, you will be a kid again."   — Sherry Torgent

"It made me laugh out loud and also brought tears to my eyes."   — A.J.

"It was one of those that I couldn't put down till it was done."   — Jeff V.

"There were moments where I realized that I had stopped breathing. There were moments that I gasped, laughed, or commented out loud."   — Ary

"This is compelling YA fiction that sets itself apart from other stories available today. It's unique, fresh, and appealing to both young women and young men. Kudos, J Washburn."   — Strykera

"It is a fun mix of fantasy and growing pains, with ominous end-of-the-world consequences." — L. Sawyer

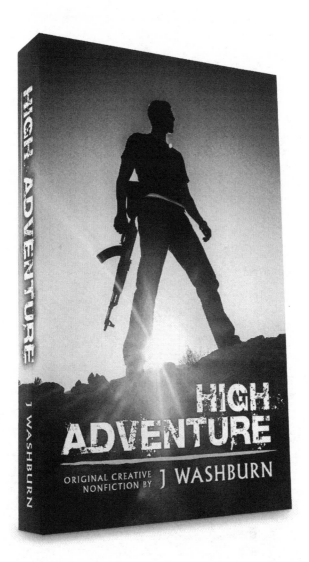

I write a monthly letter to my fans. If you subscribe to this letter at www.jwashburn.com, I'll send you a free ebook called "High Adventure."

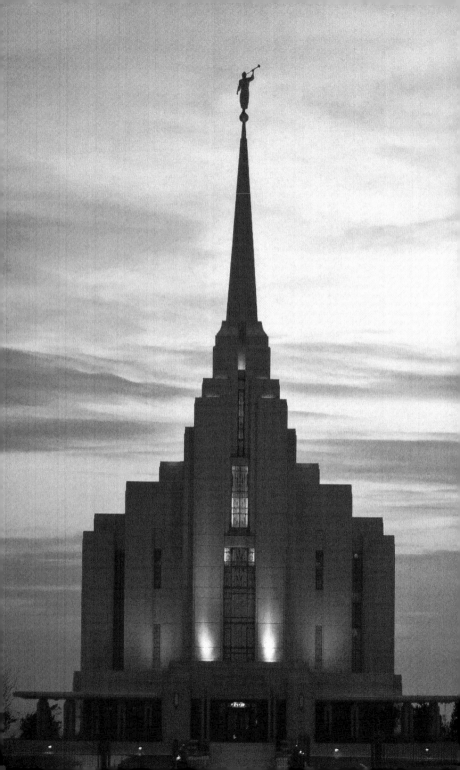

HELAMAN Gallery

Buy full-color prints of the photos from this book:
www.HelamanGallery.com

If this guide helped you,
please share it with your own
little brothers and sisters.

59280065R00142

Made in the USA
Charleston, SC
31 July 2016